# Great Power Complex

# A Socialist History of Britain

Series edited by the Northern Marxist Historians Group

# Great Power Complex
**British Imperialism, International Crises
and National Decline, 1914–51**

*John Callaghan*

Pluto Press
LONDON · CHICAGO, ILLINOIS

First published 1997 by Pluto Press
345 Archway Road, London N6 5AA
and 1436 West Randolph,
Chicago, Illinois 60607, USA

British Library Cataloguing in Publication Data
A catalogue record for his book is available from the British Library

ISBN 0 7453 1184 9 hbk

Library of Congress Cataloging in Publication Data
Callaghan, John (John T.)
    Great power complex: British imperialism, international crises,
and national decline, 1914–51/John Callaghan.
        p.   cm. — (A socialist history of Britain)
    Includes bibliographical references.
    ISBN 0–7453–1184–9
    1. Great Britain—Colonies—History—20th century.
2. Imperialism—Great Britain—History—20th century.   3. Great
Britain—Foreign relations—1910–1936.   4. Great Britain—Foreign
relations—1936–1945.   5. Great Britain—Foreign relations—1945–
I. Title.   II. Series.
DA16.C245   1997
941.082—dc21                                                    96–48789
                                                                      CIP

Designed and produced for Pluto Press by
Chase Production Services, Chadlington, OX7 3LN
Typeset from disk by Stanford DTP Services, Milton Keynes
Printed in the EC

# Contents

## List of Maps

# Acknowledgements

I would like to thank John Saville, Victor Kiernan and Roger van Zwanenberg for reading an earlier version of this text and for their constructive advice and encouragement. Responsibility for the final version remains mine alone.

# Preface

Britain's acquisition of an extensive empire was the inevitable result of its precocious emergence as a major commercial and industrial power. It was extended and consolidated on the basis of a firm economic hegemony, established in the early nineteenth century, shortly after the last of its rivals was seen off after a decades-long military campaign. The introduction to this book briefly considers the sources of this unprecedented expansion. But the main body of the book is concerned with a very different epoch which may best be described as a period of rearguard action and mismanagement, when Britain entered a period of relative economic decline, was beset by new powerful rivals, and embroiled in major wars which brought national bankruptcy. During this period of protracted crisis – a time, moreover, when opposition to imperialism was unmistakably growing within the Empire – British politicians effectively ignored the signs of national decline and persisted with the country's over-blown world role. Indeed, they used such opportunities as came their way to expand it. Persistence in error is perhaps suggestive of political incompetence, but it has also raised the question of whether successive British governments put the interests of certain sectors of the economy – notably the City of London – before those of domestic industry and the nation as a whole, and to the detriment of both.

This is not to say that the Empire was of no economic or political use to Britain in the period 1914–51; the text will make clear that in certain ways it was, though no British administration could draw up a balance sheet of costs and benefits or bothered to estimate one. The point is rather that persistence with what was an unsustainable world role, apart from drawing attention to the seeming incapacity of the political elite to imagine or consider an alternative direction for the country, ensured that the Empire – the source of Britain's 'Great Power Complex' – continued to affect the nation long after its formal dismantling.

The most obvious example of this was the way the 'imperial world-role and a gross overestimation of its own economic and political influence lay at the core of the British establishment's delusion that the United Kingdom could stand aside from European involvement'.[1] This was an issue on which it was so utterly convinced that the political elite consistently ignored and/or defied the policy of the United States which – at least until the economic crisis of the 1970s – was in favour of British participation. Of course the fact that the United States favoured Britain's involvement in the process of European integration was not allowed to disturb another delusion and one that was closely related to that of the imperial world role after 1945: namely that Britain enjoyed a 'special relationship' with the United States. As Palmer observes, the result was that 'for some thirty years Britain experienced the worst of all worlds: it no longer enjoyed any real "special relationship" with America, it was isolated outside the EEC, and it was seen by many other Europeans, in the view attributed to President de Gaulle, as little more than "America's Trojan Horse"'.[2] It was certainly so accustomed to supporting the United States in the Cold War that, while it was possible for a conservative President of France to criticise the American war in Vietnam in the 1960s, a Labour government in Britain 'was keen to demonstrate that [it] could act as the United States' main ally in policing the world'.[3] This it sought to do by supplying the United States with weapons and jungle training facilities, as well as public support for American aggresssion in Southeast Asia. One of the pay-offs of this policy was supposed to be greater influence on the policy of the United States (the 'special relationship' delusion again) and a place at the 'top table' (the world role fixation).

Labour's posture over Vietnam was linked to the main lines of British foreign policy as it had developed since the end of the Second World War when preservation of the Empire was associated with the need to involve the United States in British and European defence and reconstruction. These objectives were achieved, and initial American hostility to British imperialism was overcome, only after it was firmly established – with British encouragement of course – that international communism was the main threat to US interests. But having secured a 'partnership' role for itself in the common struggle – and, indeed, shown the way by its occupation of Greece (1944–47) – the British establishment was thereafter obliged to demonstrate in deeds the seriousness with which it bore this responsibility, a task which meant consistently bearing a heavier burden of military expenditure than other members of NATO as well as supporting America's own diplomatic and military initiatives, from the Korean War (1950–53) to the Gulf War (1991). Apart from the prolonged campaign in Vietnam (1962–75) and the invasions of the Dominican Republic (1965), Grenada (1983), and Panama (1989), the United States has been involved in at least a dozen coups and destabilisation programmes – as well as the funding of others to achieve the same effect – throughout Central and South America, the Caribbean, Middle East, Africa and

Southeast Asia. On numerous occasions British governments did what they could to support the United States up to and including direct assistance, as in the 1953 coup which overthrew the nationalist government of Mohammed Mussaddiq in Iran.[4]

In return for this loyalty British governments in the post-war years were permitted to 'decolonise' or prolong colonial rule at their own discretion. The defence of imperial interests happily coincided with war against communism in Malaya (1948–60) and led to military intervention against the democratically elected, but avowedly Marxist government of the People's Progressive Party in British Guiana in 1953 (a struggle taken over by the CIA when the PPP was re-elected in 1961). In neither of these cases would anyone expect the United States to complain about British policy. Similarly, though many reasons could be found by both governments to justify the appeasement of South Africa after it formally adopted apartheid in 1948, the anti-communist credentials of its government were readily invoked. But communism did not always supply a convenient excuse for coercive action. The savage repression used to maintain colonial rule in Kenya between 1952 and 1959 is a case in point and one that would have provoked fierce American opposition before the era of the Cold War. Even though there was no question of communism in the Kenyan case, the United States did not adopt an unduly critical stance towards British policy. In this sense the 'special relationship' was real enough; it amounted to preserving a status quo congenial for Western economic interests, even if that meant the maintenance of colonialism, client regimes and dictatorships – including those, like Franco's in Spain, that had collaborated with the fascist enemies of Britain and America during the Second World War.[5]

Britain was allowed to keep its Empire but paid the cost in terms of its disproportionate contribution to NATO as well as the preservation of an East of Suez military presence which was running at £100m per annum in 1964. By this time the architects of the main lines of Britain's post-war foreign policy had been replaced in the Labour Party by their apprentices such as Denis Healey and Patrick Gordon-Walker and a personnel that had learned zealous advocacy of the principal elements of this policy during the Cold War of the 1950s. Thus in Britain both major parties supported the 'independent nuclear deterrent', Britain's membership of NATO and its special relationship with the United States, as well as the idea of Britain as a Power capable of performing a world role. The Labour government of 1964–70 – the first for 13 years and charged with high hopes of social reform – spent over £400m per annum on military commitments overseas at a time when it was prepared to sacrifice its manifesto commitments in the interests of correcting a balance of payments deficit of just £800m. (It also undertook to modernise Polaris nuclear submarines – a project which ultimately cost £1 billion by the time of its belated deployment in the 1980s.)[6] The national economy suffered for six years during which devotion to eliminating the deficit was said to be the government's main priority; but the single largest contributor to the balance of payments deficit – military spending overseas – was maintained unimpaired.

If grandiose ideas of Britain's global significance remain a legacy of empire, the Wilson government's reluctance to devalue sterling is a reminder of another. That is the extent to which Britain's performance as a manufacturing nation has been sacrificed in the interest of securing its role as a world banker, a position it acquired during Britain's period of overseas expansion and industrial leadership. Low investment, the perennial malaise of British industry since 1945, is related to the periodic swings in government policy that have produced economic restraint whenever economic growth threatened to weaken the value of the pound. Balance of payments crises in 1947, 1949, 1951, 1955, 1957, 1961, and 1963–66 caused sterling crises because sterling was used as an international currency and foreign holders of the currency lost confidence in its ability to maintain the parity fixed against the dollar in 1949 (at £1 = $2.80).

If sterling originally acquired its global significance when Britain was the world's premier commercial and industrial power, it only retained its position as a banker's currency because of the size of the sterling trading area. This in turn owed much to the scale of British imperialism. Thus even though the British economy was no longer able to maintain 'top currency' status for sterling, the pound remained a 'master currency' on the strength of empire from 1932, when the sterling area was created out of the ruins of international recession and the collapse of the gold standard. But the relative weakness of the British economy after 1945 inevitably generated periodic panics about the value of its currency. The restoration of confidence in sterling invariably entailed the government in raising interest rates and taxes, and introducing measures to reduce demand; but these measures were also guaranteed to slow domestic growth rates and undermine confidence in the viability of long-term investment plans in Britain. The fact that a significant proportion of British industry was globally oriented (including a dispropor-tionately large number of multinational companies) – itself a legacy of empire – meant that leading businesses had the option of expanding their overseas interests instead of investing in 'stop–go' Britain, and this merely exacerbated the tendency for low investment and productivity in the domestic economy. The result was that until the collapse of the sterling area in 1967, the value of the pound had to be geared to its international role rather than the needs of an ailing domestic manufacturing sector.[7]

The British Empire, in short, casts a long shadow over recent British history. Numerous issues in British politics are related to it, from the scale and operation of the arms industry to the war over the Falklands/Malvinas in April 1982. Britain's decline as a world power was inevitable, but the fact that it became 'one of the weakest and least successful of the second rate powers'[8] was not – it was in part a consequence of refusing to acknowledge that its Great Power days were over.

*The British Empire in 1815*

New South Wales

Van Diemen's Land

Andaman Islands

Penang Island

Ceylon

Bencoolen

Cocos Islands

India

Laccadive Islands

Maldive Islands

Seychelles Islands

Mauritius Islands

Ionian Islands

Heligoland

Malta

Cape Colony

British Isles

Gibraltar

Gold Coast

Gambia

Sierra Leone

Ascension Island

St Helena

Tristan da Cunha

Labrador

Newfoundland

Lower Canada (Quebec)

Bermuda

Bahamas

Jamaica

Trinidad

British Guiana

Rupert's Land

Selkirk Colony

Upper Canada (Ontario)

British Honduras

Pitcairn Island

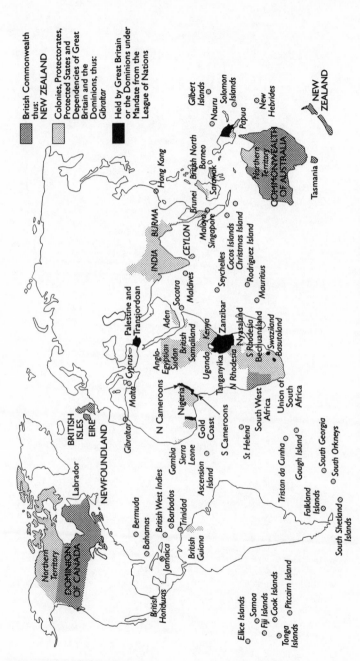

British Empire and Commonwealth in 1939

Legend:

British Commonwealth
thus:
NEW ZEALAND

Colonies, Protectorates,
Protected States and
Dependencies of Great
Britain and the
Dominions, thus:
*Gibraltar*

Held by Great Britain
or the Dominions under
Mandate from the
League of Nations

# Introduction: The Expansion of England

Before proceeding with our examination of British imperial policy in the period of its prolonged crisis we need to have some idea of how and why Britain's overseas expansion occurred. The short answer is that the British state engaged its leading economic opponents in a succession of wars – the Dutch in the seventeenth century, the French in the eighteenth – and emerged from these conflicts with an enlarged economic power as well as new overseas possessions.

It is a commonplace of international relations theory that once nation-states began to emerge, each pursuing its own interests, the very structure of the international system became a factor in their competition, since the national security of any one state depended on preparation for war, and this inevitably bred insecurity elsewhere and reactive measures in kind. In the past, much more than the present, the absence of nation-states in much of the world (and the decay of older centres of power) left many other peoples exposed to the depredations of the well-armed. In other words those without a centralised power were vulnerable – as the inhabitants of Africa, India, and China were to discover – to the incursions of those who had this facility. 'From about the twelfth to the nineteenth century, between 70 and 90 per cent of the English state's financial resources were continuously devoted to the acquisition and use of the instruments of military force, especially in international wars.' In the seventeenth and eighteenth centuries the absolute size of this military expenditure grew enormously and 'the state's real finances grew rapidly, largely in response to the escalating costs of the means of "coercive power"; in this case, the costs of growing, professional, standing armies and navies'.[1]

The intensification of state rivalries which this military expansion both signified and exacerbated, was intimately related to the emergence of a world economy. The dominant forces, in this context, were those states able to raise the requisite economic resources to exclude their rivals from overseas markets and sources of raw materials, food and cheap labour. The expansion overseas of these states was both evidence of their economic power (made possible by prior political and technological advances) and a means to further augment it. By the seventeenth century the English state

1

was already in a position to play a leading part in the developing world system; it was a major trading power and one that was well practised and fully committed to a policy of using military power against its commercial rivals. The maritime wars which England fought against Holland in 1652–54, 1665–67, and 1672–74 were essentially a struggle for commercial supremacy between the two leading trading nations of Europe. All the wars of the next 150 years had an economic purpose.

The architects of English (after 1707 British) policy were members of a ruling bloc composed of the aristocracy and monarchy, together with the merchants and bankers of London. All the elements of this elite were proponents and beneficiaries of the commercial-military policy to which we have alluded. Changes in the political regime during the seventeenth century – such as the passage from Charles I to Cromwell and later to the restored monarchy – did not affect the issue.

> Not only did the merchants interested in these measures retain their influence over the government: the tradition of economic policy established in the interregnum actually became stronger after the Restoration. The newly revived factor in English policy, the court, joined in it with the City. Princes, ministers, and the members of their circle took shares in the great joint-stock companies and saw to it that these got at least such naval and military help as could be conveniently spared ... Thus the leading naval and military administrators were personally interested in commercial and colonial expansion, and soon after the Restoration they hoped to hasten that expansion by disputing the power of the Dutch.[2]

After the Glorious Revolution of 1688 the aristocracy, a class well on its way to becoming a capitalist stratum in its own right, controlled affairs in England through Parliament. But they did so in harmony with the interests of the merchant and financial oligarchy of the City of London. Indeed in the wake of 1688 a financial revolution established the modern institutional foundations of the City. The Bank of England (1694) and the national debt were created; a practical gold standard was developed; specialised merchant banks and insurance services arose and the stock exchange was established (by the 1820s).

Together these fractions of English capital pursued the policy of overseas conquest and extracted whatever taxes were required to finance its main instrument – the navy. Cain and Hopkins observe that:

> the social incidence of taxation identifies the chief beneficiaries of the Revolution Settlement: the landed interest, which voted

itself valuable tax benefits; the bond-holders in London and the Home Counties, who gained from transfers made by taxpayers in the country as a whole; and the merchants trading overseas (in association with shipowners, contractors and members of the armed services), who profited from the drive to increase earnings and revenues from the colonies.[3]

By the middle of the eighteenth century their policy of aggressive overseas expansion had transformed London into the largest centre of international trade in the world.

Indeed it has been argued that 'a fundamental reason why Britain was not torn apart by civil war after 1688 was that its inhabitants' aggression was channelled so regularly and so remorselessly into war and imperial expansion abroad'.[4]

Success, above all success in war, was what the men who governed Great Britain were able to hold out as a legitimisation of their rule to the millions below them. The Nine Years War with France, the War of Spanish Succession, the wars of Jenkins' Ear and the Austrian Succession, the Seven Years War and the wars against Revolutionary and Napoleonic France, all brought enough military and naval victories in their train to flatter British pride, and in most of these conflicts the victories were not only massive but durable in terms of empire won and trade routes gained.[5]

Imperialism thus played a part in reinforcing elite privileges against the incipient challenge of the lower orders – no more so than during periods of political turbulence such as those that followed the French Revolution of 1789. The successful policy of overseas expansion also greatly contributed to cementing the elements of the British ruling class and contributing to that harmony between the landed aristocracy and the commercial and financial interests of the country which became one of its hallmarks. All of these fractions of the ruling class benefited from the ruthless struggle for colonial markets and the ultimate defeat of their principal imperial and commercial rivals; just as the landed were enriched by trade, the traders needed the military might – particularly the naval reach – that underwrote trade and its rapid expansion. By the late eighteenth century, 'monarchy, army, navy, militia and empire were coming to be fused in a new kind of patriotism, which united rather than divided upper-class opinion'.[6]

By that time too the British had established a superior financial system which enabled the state to 'spend on war out of all proportion to its tax revenue'.[7] Britain's financial advantages stemmed in part from the fact that per capita income was already higher than in France by 1700 and by the Napoleonic Wars the state was able to raise greater annual tax revenues (from the mass of consumers) than its more populous neighbour. Furthermore, the British state possessed a decisive advantage in its ability to raise loans. It not only drew on the credit made possible by a prospering banking system and stock exchange, but gained a reputation for credit-worthiness based on the state's ability to meet its obligations. Sound public finances were in turn at least partly dependent on the growth in public revenues derived from the expansion of trade and industry, as well as Parliament's ability to raise additional taxes when necessary. 'The result of all this was not only that interest rates steadily dropped but also that British government stock was increasingly attractive to foreign, and particularly Dutch, investors. In *power-political* terms, its value lay in the way in which the resources of the United Provinces repeatedly came to the aid of the British war effort ...'[8] Napoleonic France suffered the misfortune, moreover, that its protracted confrontation with Britain occurred when the first industrial revolution was well underway and the mounting costs of war were that much easier for Britain to bear.

One important sign of this was that the British already possessed the biggest arms export trade in the world by the time of the French wars. Bayly tells us that 'it had swamped Asia and America with sophisticated muskets' and that armaments exports and related subsidies were an important component of Britain's wartime diplomacy. Moreover, 'the export of the British arms surplus between 1804 and 1824 played a critical part in arming the forces of the state at an international level and ensuring its victory over internal dissidents, peasant rebels and armed plunderers'.[9] The British ruling class now stood for order and sought allies abroad with the same interest in averting radical departures to republican democracy. The wars against revolutionary France saw the propertied class in Britain close ranks in defence of the political status quo, finding as they did so that religion, monarchy and patriotism were potent instruments for mobilising substantial popular forces behind them. Britain was poised to play the role of world policeman which its emerging economic hegemony both demanded and facilitated. No interest had a bigger stake in international 'stability' than the City of London.

After 1815 the financial primacy of the City was established on the basis of industrial revolution and undisputed British mastery of the seas. Amsterdam, so recently Britain's financier and the City's superior, never recovered from the wartime blockade together with the massive preponderance of British manufacturing which the conflict with France helped to promote. By the end of the protracted struggle, Britain had acquired numerous additional overseas bases from its enemies, thus securing the 'influence' which it needed in order to drag new areas into the world economy which it now dominated. Strategic positions were acquired in Heligoland, Malta, the Ionian Islands, Mauritius, the Seychelles, Ceylon, Malacca, St Lucia and Tobago, Guiana, Ascension, Gambia and Sierra Leone. In short, Britain held dominating positions in every ocean of the world with the exception of the Pacific and useful points from which access to bigger territories could be effected.

There can be no denying the contribution of colonies to Britain's industrial might, though they were by no means a sufficient condition for its economic transformation into 'the workshop of the world'.[10] This contribution took numerous forms. It can be seen from the fact that '95 per cent of *the increase* in Britain's commodity exports that occurred in the six decades after the Act of Union [in 1707] was sold to captive and colonial markets outside Europe' and re-exports of colonial goods 'made up almost 40 per cent of total British exports ...'.[11] Hyam also points out that 'without the capture of the Indian, Chinese, and South-East Asian inter-port trade in the thirty years before 1815, without the position built up in the "carrying trades" in Asian primary products (tea, opium, raw cotton, spices, and tin), Britain would not have been able so rapidly later to develop the sale of her manufactured textiles in the east as she did'.[12] We can go back even further of course. Among the great and expanding patterns of trade up to the industrial revolution was the triangular trade across the Atlantic in West African slaves, Caribbean and American raw materials and foodstuffs and British manufactures. Bristol, Liverpool and Glasgow grew directly from this trade and the expansion of the Lancashire cotton industry would be hard to explain without reference to it. In the nineteenth century, however, the school of political economy inspired by Adam Smith denounced the mercantilist 'old colonial system' altogether and the slave trade was soon to be thought of as a morally and economically discredited survivor of the old mentality which unnecessarily restricted the growth of trade and prosperity. But it was conveniently overlooked that it also played a role in the crude accumulation of capital that preceded the industrial revolution:

> The discovery of gold and silver in America, the extirpation, enslavement and entombment in mines of the aboriginal population, the beginning of the conquest and looting of the East Indies, the turning of Africa into a warren for the commercial hunting of black skins, signalised the rosy dawn of the era of capitalist production. These idyllic proceedings are the chief momenta of primitive accumulation.[13]

The new school of economists notwithstanding, the conviction persisted that dominion entailed wealth as well as power. Edmund Burke, Whig politician and political theorist of conservatism, was not alone when he reasoned that commerce could be 'united with,

and made to flourish by war'.[14] British actions testified to the
durability of this belief throughout the nineteenth century. Even
when its commercial and industrial lead was assured, it continued
to add to its overseas possessions; such actions led to the taking of
Singapore (1819), the Falkland Islands (1833), Aden (1839),
Hong Kong (1841) and later still bases in Lagos, Fiji, Cyprus,
Alexandria, Mombasa and Zanzibar. Expansion was not, however,
the simple result of state-initiated violence; the commercial drive
to expansion was integral to capitalism from its beginnings and it
was the dynamic of British economic expansion which increasingly
lay at the root of things. In the period 1815–70, Britain's pre-eminent
power rested on its unique industrial strength and on this basis it
dominated trade, transport and finance. This is what enabled the
City and the Bank of England to supply short-term credit for the
world economy; the actual volume of sterling transactions grew
immensely as Britain held a virtual monopoly of manufactures,
shipping and colonies.

It was the rivalries of the several leading commercial powers in
the seventeenth and eighteenth centuries which made the role of
the state conspicuous as an instrument of conquest and the defence
of conquests, and the provider of trade monopolies and other
mercantilist arrangements designed to secure exclusive control
and enrichment to the nation-state. But after the elimination of its
surviving European rival, France, in 1815 – a struggle which led
to 'the greatest expansion of British imperial dominion since the
creation of the colonies of settlement' in the seventeenth century[15]
– the British became wedded to the ideology of free trade in the
context of the commercial superiority which its developing industrial
power and the new power-political vacuum vouchsafed. Steps
were taken to erect the new economic order as soon as the war ended.
Public spending was cut, the gold standard was revived and by the
1820s tariffs were being cut. Military force and further conquest
could now play a far less conspicuous role for much of the rest of
the nineteenth century and it was easier for the British to delude
themselves under these circumstances into thinking that their real
mission was to bring civilisation to barbaric peoples,[16] thus masking
the fact that their primary motivation had been to enrich themselves
through overseas conquest and exploitation.[17] This indeed remained
the case as the British state came to identify with the new conditions
associated with its pre-eminence: free trade, the operation of the
domestic gold standard and a prolonged peace on British terms (the
*Pax Britannica*) which its naval might supervised across the globe.

Clearly, in fact, both the foundation and much of the purpose
of Britain's formal dominion overseas rested on direct coercion.
Empires are not based upon consent. By the time the slave trade

was abolished in the British Empire in 1807, for example, Britain had exported over three million Africans into slavery and it continued to make use of slave labour and indentured labour for much longer. Even after the emancipation of slaves in the Caribbean (1833), the exploitation of various forms of directly coerced workers such as indentured migrants from India – shipped in their hundreds of thousands to Mauritius, the Caribbean, East and South Africa and Fiji – continued unabated. State violence likewise remained an instrument for obtaining and keeping markets, as when Britain went to war with China in 1839–42, and again in 1856–58 (thereby bringing it into the informal Empire) to enforce the sale of opium. Ministers of state could sometimes be perfectly open about the commercial motivations involved in conquest and annexation as Lord Randolph Churchill was when Upper Burma was taken by force in January 1886.[18] Obviously, competitors could be excluded by means of annexations; but direct control also enabled the imperial power to establish its own commercial rules among the occupied peoples. Such rules might involve the elimination of rival sources of supply as in the destruction of the Indian textile industry (a victim of crippling tariffs and the Navigation Acts as well as superior technology); or they might entail compulsory consumption of a product, such as the enforced wearing of woollen and cotton clothing by Africans in Natal (duly supplied by British industry) .

But imperialism was not just about annexations and the formal subjugation of overseas territories. The exercise of power over other peoples which lies at the heart of imperialism could be effected without imposing formal instruments of direct rule. Since what really mattered was the ability of the British ruling class to impose its will in order to secure benefits for itself – whether these were economic, strategic or whatever – and maintain this structure of inequality in its relations with overseas countries, imperialism could function perfectly well on an informal basis if these objectives could be secured by means of treaties, the installation of client regimes, the purchase of cooperation from local elites and so on. Indeed in the era of free trade imperialism, Britain's economic and military superiority was such that its decision-making elite was more confident that these informal devices for the establishment of commercial rules beneficial to itself would suffice, and thus relieve the British state of bearing certain costs associated with the maintenance of colonies. During the parliamentary debate to repeal the Corn Laws in 1846, one supporter of free trade argued precisely this. Free trade, he said, was the principle by which 'foreign nations would become valuable colonies to us, without imposing on us the responsibility of governing them'.[19] Nevertheless, colonies were never surrendered and new possessions continued to be added to the existing imperial 'burden' even in the decades when the ideology of free trade rose towards its zenith.

Revolts of colonial subjects or those who threatened to disturb the rules of British trade in its wider sphere of influence were 'invariably put down ruthlessly ... often ... with a rampage of cultural destruction, such as occurred in Jogjakarta (Java) in 1812, Kandy in 1818 and Peking in 1858 ...'. Hyman informs us that 'the Kandy revolt of 1817–18 was put down ferociously. Perhaps 10,000 Singhalese died. The British burned and terrorised, starved the population and destroyed houses, crops, cattle, and fruit trees.'[20] In this period of its economic and strategic dominance, Britain's military supremacy could nevertheless be had on the cheap; the subjugated could be kept in their place by gunboats (though the off-shore presence of the fleet usually sufficed), while major military rivals simply did not materialise before the 1870s. Nevertheless, every effort was made to minimise the costs of imperial rule and everywhere they could, the British relied on local collaborators – usually the traditional elites – to govern the places of informal dominion as well as some of the more massive territories of formal rule such as India. Despite its burgeoning industrial power and comfortable economic supremacy in the first half of the nineteenth century, however, no British statesmen of the first rank ever suggested the abandonment of the colonial Empire. On the contrary, new possessions were added between mid-century and the 1870s (before, in other words, the 'scramble for Africa' of the 1880s and 1890s inaugurated the so-called 'new imperialism'); Lower Burma, Kowloon, the Transvaal, and Basutoland were among the acquisitions of this period.

As late as the 1860s Britain's was the only industrial economy in the world and in this its Golden Age the Royal Navy patrolled the oceans, securing the trade routes to the outposts of the formal empire (in India, Canada, Australasia, the Cape and Natal, British Guiana and the Caribbean) and enforcing British terms of trade on an informal dominion which ranged from the Atlantic to the China Sea, with the assistance of the expanding chain of island bases and strategic ports already mentioned. Despite its massive lead in manufactures, the consensus in the political class was that Britain still required its overseas possessions. The Empire had many uses and many individuals profited personally from it, including leading politicians.[21] Empire had always assisted the supply of cheap essential raw materials and foodstuffs to Britain – so it was perceived as all the more essential when the policy of free trade weakened British agriculture in practice from the last quarter of the nineteenth century. The politicians also believed that Empire provided the safety-valve of ridding Britain of its 'surplus population', as numerous state-assisted emigration schemes attest well into the twentieth century. Until the 1860s it also provided penal settlements in Australasia that can best be likened to slave-labour concentration camps.[22] Empire also provided troops, notably Indian troops which were used in China (1839, 1856, and 1859), Persia (1856), Ethiopia (1867), Afghanistan (1878), Egypt (1882), Burma (1885), Nyasaland (1893) the Sudan and Uganda (1896),[23] to mention only a sample of the occasions on which they were deployed. It was, in short, considered a versatile asset by the overwhelming majority of the political class – most of whom, no doubt, were not careful to distinguish between its commercial, financial, strategic, political, social and recreational benefits.

In the period of its unchallenged dominance, 1815–70, Britain enjoyed the benefits of a system of reinforcing parts. Elements of this system had been in operation for some time, as we have seen. Naval victories had assisted Britain's merchants in the eighteenth century and military success rested to a significant extent on a superior financial system, which in turn derived from the expansion of trade and the possession of colonies. To this virtuous circle was added industrialisation from the end of the eighteenth century, which 'not only furthered the British ascendancy in commerce and finance and shipping [but] also underpinned its own naval supremacy with a previously unheard-of economic potential'.[24] By the middle of the nineteenth century Britain produced two-thirds of the world's coal, manufactured five-sevenths of its steel, was mining half its iron and selling half of its commercial cloth. Its trade expanded so rapidly that as it did so the City became the clearing-house for the world economy and centre for all aspects of international finance. Free trade was the logical choice for a country so far ahead of its rivals in all things economic. But for an island economy such as Britain's – massively dependent on trade and covering no great land area – the retention of its global network of strategically sited naval bases was just as commonsensical. As Kennedy observes, the equation on which British power rested consisted of an

> overwhelming world naval force ... an expanding formal empire ... together with a far larger informal empire, both of which provided essential raw materials and markets for the British economy; and an industrial revolution which poured out its products into the rest of the world, drew large overseas territories into its commercial and financial orbit, encouraged an enormous merchant marine, and provided the material strength to support its great fleets.[25]

But the *Pax Britannica* ultimately depended on the inability of would-be rivals to challenge the British hegemony. During the first half of the nineteenth century the chief contenders lagged behind industrially, were preoccupied with nation-building and beset by

internal social conflicts that threatened to tear them apart. These
states – Germany and the United States were the first to catch up
with Britain – never accepted the British doctrine of free trade and
sought instead to nurture their own infant industries behind
protective tariffs. When the challenge to Britain materialised in the
1880s – with both France and Germany clamouring for colonies
– Britain's response was to protect what it held by fresh annexations
and 'the scramble for Africa' commenced. In the event Britain took
the greater part of the territories that were now seized and the formal
empire expanded enormously in the 1880s and 1890s. Thus just
when its informal power was being cut back by the expansion of
its industrialising rivals, Britain's formal dominion expanded. Yet
Britain's manufacturing supremacy was over, as the industrial
growth of the United States and Germany demonstrated by the time
of the 1881 census. Other countries were also catching up and eating
into Britain's share of world trade. Global dominion was perforce
at an end. As this inevitably shrank, however, Britain's overseas
interests came to be more and more equated with the preservation
of the formal empire – the annexed territories that were coloured
red on the map. In reality this was also problematic. Before the
century was over it was no longer self-evident – as the second Boer
War (1899–1902) attested – that Britain had the resources to
defend this object of increasing national glorification.

The ability to exercise direct or indirect control over far-flung
possessions had always been the necessary precondition of Britain's
overseas expansion, as we have seen. By the end of the nineteenth
century, however, both the economic and the military preconditions
of the *Pax Britannica* had already been lost. Economic and military
rivals had appeared. Britain was more dependent than any of them
on overseas supplies of food and raw materials. It was therefore
potentially vulnerable in times of war. Its rivals, on the other hand,
covered greater land masses and had always been careful to protect
their own industries by tariffs. They denounced free trade, moreover,
as a British hypocrisy while taking advantage of it to penetrate the
British home market. Not surprisingly, therefore, the challenge to
British hegemony which developed in the last two decades of the
nineteenth century spurred elements within Britain to question the
country's commercial, military and imperial policy. An argument
was fashioned, in particular, that the British could only maintain
their power in the face of the growing challenge represented by
Germany and the United States by the creation of a much more
cohesive empire in defence of Anglo-Saxon interests. By the end
of the century Joseph Chamberlain was the acknowledged leader
inside the Conservative Party of this movement for tariff reform
and imperial federation, and the Tories had now become the
political expression of big property in all its forms (commercial,

financial, industrial, landed). Chamberlain's policy of creating a self-sufficient protectionist bloc was ultimately defeated, as we shall see (it is not too much to say that it was utterly unrealistic in any case). But the forebodings which led to the rise of this programme within the Conservative Party were real enough. The capitalist world system had entered a period of instability that would culminate in the First World War.

# CHAPTER 1

# Imperialist War, 1914–18

The period 1914 to 1951 was a period of enormous turmoil in world politics which was set on its course by the most decisive event of the twentieth century – the First World War. It behoves us briefly to consider the nature of this conflict before we go any further and to ask in particular if the war can be understood in terms of imperialism.

It was a war largely fought by imperialist powers, especially the British, French, Tsarist, Austro-Hungarian, German and Ottoman Empires. It was a war fought with the resources of empires. These resources were sometimes mobilised with the aid of coercion or with promises of some future improvement in the condition of subject peoples. The promises, most of them broken, stored up problems for the future. But even when imperial resources were mobilised with the genuine support of certain elements within the subject peoples, the war generated destabilising effects. It changed economies and social structures, made excessive demands and raised expectations. In the minds of imperialists the war generated anxieties of another sort; all sorts of decisions – from the pros and cons of retreat from Gallipoli to the question of support for 'one last big push' in the West (Passchendaele) – were taken with at least one eye on their expected imperial ramifications, including the all-important commodity of imperial prestige.

In the British case the imperial contribution to the war was extensive, involving two and a half million colonial troops and hundreds of thousands of carriers and other non-combatant helpers.[1] The colonies also supplied money and material, including raw materials vital for the war effort. The theatres of war included the colonial territories of the leading combatants and campaigns were waged to divest rivals of these possessions; in this way Germany was dispossessed in the Pacific and East Africa, while the Turks were forced to give up the dominions of the Ottoman Empire in the Middle East. Parts of Britain's 'informal empire' – always something of an imposture in any case – were annexed (like Cyprus) or unilaterally declared protectorates and turned into a militarised zone (like Egypt). The war, in short, was imperialist in all these ways and permanently altered the imperial map. The British Empire survived – indeed expanded – while others collapsed, but the costs were high both in terms of money and permanently altered imperial relationships. Britain emerged not only with its money capital depleted but with considerably reduced moral capital as well.

Yet the war undoubtedly heightened the perception of the Empire's value to Great Britain, at least within the business and political elites of the country. It could hardly do otherwise given the extreme national emergency and the heightened awareness in governing circles of all those imperial assets which were now deployed in Britain's potentially ruinous struggle against the Central Powers. The new sense of empire was proclaimed, however, as more than just a short-term expedient. The war instilled new life into the old Chamberlainite visions of imperial federation and rekindled hopes of national aggrandisement through a more systematic exploitation of imperial resources. An Indian Industrial Commission was appointed in 1916, for example, which recommended a conscious policy of rapid industrialisation on the subcontinent. It was a novel departure from *laissez-faire* and derived credibility at the time from the quickened tempo of economic change in India induced by the circumstances of war. But there was more to it than the observation of fact. The keener imperialists, the men touched by the Chamberlainite afflatus, found themselves propelled into the highest reaches of the government – the more as the war went on. These were men like Arthur Balfour, Edward Carson, George Nathaniel Curzon, Alfred Milner and Jan Smuts, supported by younger enthusiasts such as Leo Amery, Mark Sykes, Waldorf Astor, Philip Kerr and Lionel Curtis – the last three of whom belonged to Lloyd George's personal secretariat. Here were the prophets of national efficiency and national survival through the mechanism of empire. They were supported in this orientation, as Bernard Porter points out, 'from a dozen quarters – ... from a Dominions Royal Commission ... from an unofficial "Empire Resources Development Committee" formed in 1917, and from a host of pamphleteers and propagandists ... [who produced] ... a flood of proposals during the war, reminiscent of the great Joe, to exploit the empire like an estate under siege ...'.[2]

These visionaries were members of one of the lobbies which had done so much mischief in embittering relations between the Great Powers since the mid-1880s. In all the imperialist countries, imperialist rhetoric formed an important part of the Right's domestic self-promotion, in particular its trumpeting of patriotism and its exposure of the lack of it in its political rivals, particularly the socialists. Political opportunism found governments rehearsing their chants of chauvinism, racism and xenophobia as circumstances allowed – and there was no shortage of occasions when such sentiments were usefully evoked. In this way the political mainstream joined forces with the dogmatic agitations of committed imperialists in shaping important components of public opinion to look favourably on the 'unique' civilising mission and cultural superiority of this or that imperialist power. Pressure groups such as the Navy League (and, in Germany, the Pan-German League) did not fail to present their own projects in chauvinistic, racist and xenophobic terms; nor did national leaders of imperialism such as Chamberlain, Milner, and Rhodes. From the 1890s a mass-circulation press exemplified by Alfred Harmsworth's *Daily Mail* in Great Britain 'gloried in the vulgarities' of imperialism, amplified the jingo chorus and thus reinforced the nationalist and racist prejudices of its lower-middle-class readership.[3] As Joseph Schumpeter observed in 1919, all of this was very 'conspicuous to foreigners' and 'most welcome to many political parties on the Continent' with a nationalist and imperialist agenda of their own.[4]

Racism pervaded bourgeois society and was given full vent in the organs of the Right. Levels of civilisation were explained in terms of race – racial distinctions being found among the European peoples as well as between the 'imperial races' and those they had conquered.[5] The most important pseudo-scientific rationale for this ideology was social Darwinism, an influential variant of which depicted the struggle for survival as a contest between nations, presenting empires as both the result of natural selection and proof of racial superiority. These were fashionable ideas at the turn of the century and for those who subscribed to them – and a great many influential men did in all the imperialist countries – 'warfare was presented, not only as an unavoidable feature of international life, but also as something inherently desirable, since it helped to develop a courageous and resourceful community'.[6] This view – later associated with fascism – was the common property of imperialists, German or British, French or Japanese. Irrationalism ran deep in imperialist circles. As Paul Kennedy has pointed out, 'a Social Darwinistic tone ... permeate[d] virtually all the writings of ... imperialist politicians and intellectuals' in the quarter century before 1914.[7] War for such people was an opportunity to demonstrate the superiority, say, of Teutons over Slavs, and when it came in 1914 it was fought with an appropriate savagery – against civilian populations and with genocidal intent against insubordinate ethnic minorities, as in the infamous massacres of Armenians and Serbs. To find a comparable level of violence against civilian populations before 1914 – leaving aside the slaughter of 25,000 Communards – one has to turn to the atrocities committed in the Belgian Congo or the concerted suppression of the Boxer Rebellion by the imperialist powers in China.

It is no part of the present argument to suggest that imperialist ideologies, for all the hate and bellicosity they contained, actually caused the First World War. But they did provide the lens through which a significant proportion of politicians and European publics interpreted events and viewed the world, and to this extent they represent an active factor in the history of the period. They contributed, for example, to that fatalism and enthusiasm for war between the Great Powers which is present in the voluminous writings on this subject that littered the first decade of the century. But imperialism contributed to the explosive situation in more palpable ways too. The very alliance system which helped bring the war about was in part the product of agreements designed to settle colonial disputes, as in the Entente Cordiale (1904) between Britain and France and in Britain's agreement with Russia in 1907. Colonial disputes also generated a war climate or expectation of war, as when Britain and France combined to block Germany's claim for a port on the Moroccan coast in 1911. Germany's territorial and military ambitions were many of course, as befitted its burgeoning economic might in an age when states supposed that national power depended on an extensive formal hegemony. Needless to say, those Germans who accepted this equation could only feel confirmed in their opinion by the nervous reaction such aspirations occasioned in their British counterparts.

For the growth of German economic power had been a cause for anxiety in imperialist circles in Britain from the 1870s. The falling rates of profit and overcapacity of the Great Depression (1873–96) formed the context, furthermore, for a new emphasis on imperialism as a solution to a wide variety of problems: for new markets, investment opportunities, export of the 'surplus population', paying for social reform to contain the socialists and so on. In this way the colonial rivalries of the 1880s were 'to a considerable extent to grow out of the economic anxieties of the previous decade'.[8] They were also connected to the fact that the imperialist aspirations of the latecomers almost everywhere ran up against the already massive extent of the British Empire. This problem was compounded by the British predilection for regarding territories adjacent to the formal empire as of exclusive strategic significance to themselves – a board-game logic which gave the British an ever-expanding imperial interest. The spate of annexations in Africa during the 1890s was both cause and effect of a competitive imperialist dynamic which involved strategic calculations of this sort, with considerations of some possible future commercial or diplomatic benefit – as yet unknown – at the back of the imperial mind. Then there was always the simple desire to block the ubiquitous intrigues of rivals as a motive for fresh annexations. The rather relaxed, informal imperialism which the British had enjoyed at the height of their commercial and economic hegemony had to die in these circumstances, as competitors annexed their way into areas hitherto extraneous to the world economy.

The scepticism that had made Karl Marx wonder in 1857 whether 'this dominion [India] does not threaten to cost quite as much as it can ever be expected to come to'[9] was thus virtually extinguished in policy-making circles by the 1880s. Even at mid-century, however, imperialist wars and annexations had hardly constituted exceptions, notwithstanding the greater volume of scepticism expressed within the political elite. Imperialism had always been primarily an economic process incorporating new territories into the world economy on a subordinate basis and formal political domination had always been one of its features. It was simply that the British dominance of mid-century had been untroubled by serious competition and had thus been able to rest on extensive informal arrangements. Under these circumstances the doctrines of free trade and *laissez-faire* acquired the status of holy writ. By the late 1880s, in conditions of intensified competition, however, formal control looked more necessary than ever before, particularly as the latecomers like Germany were convinced practitioners of economic protectionism at home and could be expected to extend the principle to their overseas possessions.

Both political parties in Britain took steps to tighten controls over the informal empire when necessary. From the mid-1880s both contained a growing number of advocates of closer imperial association; nobody of any significance in these parties advocated withdrawal from Empire. As we saw in the introduction, in large measure Britain's world-wide imperium was both the result and chief support of its mercantile expansion and the commercial dominance consolidated by 1815. British politicians had had plenty of time to acquire the habit of empire and by the 1880s Tory demagogues such as Lord Randolph Churchill were pleased to justify new acquisitions in explicitly commercial terms. Though its costs and benefits could hardly be computed with any accuracy, it remained rational, as the nineteenth century closed, to suppose that the country's comparative advantage required the defence and maintenance of these far-flung possessions, if not their extension. The rise of powerful competitors and an emerging international oligopoly of states could only reinforce the point. It is quite unrealistic to imagine that all of this could be separate and apart from the armaments race and the war-plans of the 1900s. In preparing to fight, Britain prepared to hold on to what it had.

In the end the Anglo-German antagonism was structured by the economic expansion of Germany and the perception on both sides of the challenge that this entailed to British power. This was true even of the localised disputes involving the two countries. As Kennedy explains:

What is common to almost all of the colonial disputes is that they were the consequences – unintended perhaps yet inevitable – of *economic* expansionism. The same long-term processes which were causing many British merchants and investors to shift their gaze from Europe to the 'underdevloped' world were also responsible for German penetration of those same regions.[10]

But over and above that, the very fact of Germany's rise put British power on the defensive. The British state – a patrician monopoly – could hardly fail to see the strategic and commercial issues in this challenge. Nor were they without support from the dismal science; as Semmel notes, an extensive body of Victorian political economy 'insisted upon a chronic need, whether immediate or in the future, of the industrial system for empire' and of the need for 'the use of national power to extend and protect foreign and colonial commerce and investment'.[11] These views could only seem the more apposite in the face of growing international intolerance of the *Pax Britannica* and the erosion of the open trading system for which it had stood as guarantor. The temptation to see the future in terms of rival politico-economic blocs grew stronger. The legend 'Made in Germany' stimulated the 'commonsense' of those who believed that global resources and wealth were fixed or who took the view that there was no domestic solution to the unemployed 'residuum' or the even bigger probem of the 'social question'.

When a European war finally ignited, Britain was bound to become involved because as Sir Edward Grey, the Foreign Secretary, told the American Ambassador in London:

> The issue for us is that, if Germany wins, she will dominate France; the independence of Belgium, Holland, Denmark, and perhaps of Norway and Sweden, will be a mere shadow; their separate existence as nations will be a fiction; all their harbours will be at Germany's disposal; she will dominate the whole of Western Europe, and this will make our position quite impossible. We could not exist as a first class State under such circumstances.[12]

Although the talk here is of Europe, Britain's status as a Power was inseparable from its imperial might in the minds of men like Grey. British imperial power would not long survive if Germany dominated Europe. The military might of nations was well understood to depend on their economic power and both military and economic might were perceived to be inextricably bound up with imperialism – not only in the minds of the British, but in those of all the other Powers too. Grey's calculation was soon confirmed. In May 1915 the six most powerful economic groupings in Germany petitioned the Chancellor to demand extensive territorial annexations once the war was won. These were to include Belgium, much of the English Channel coastline of France, its northern coalfields, the granaries of Eastern Europe, and colonial acquisitions, in the words of the petitioners, 'adequate to satisfy Germany's manifold economic interests' – and presumably at the expense of Britain and France.[13]

Even after four years of futile slaughter, the appetite for imperialism remained as keen as ever and plans for fresh territorial annexations and dismemberments – considered on a virtually continuous basis as the war raged – were now ready for implementation. Everywhere the war was publicly fought in self-defence against authoritarian aggressors; the needs of mass mobilisation and popular legitimacy demanded no less. Behind the scenes, however, deals were done to allow Russia to annex the Straits and Constantinople, to possess Armenia, Kurdistan and Poland; so that France could repossess Alsace-Lorraine, take Syria, the Saar and the left bank of the Rhine; to allow Britain to control Transjordan, Palestine and Mesopotamia and take over most of Germany's African colonies. Italy, Japan, Romania, Greece, Bulgaria – a long queue of states – expected their own territorial prizes. Germany, of course, ended up with nothing. But as in Britain, the war had the effect of heightening the significance of imperialism and removing any objections which had restrained its extremists before August 1914. Under these conditions the formulation of war aims at governmental level involved massive territorial annexations in Europe and Africa, as already noted, and though these were thwarted in 1918 they were later revived by the Nazis.[14] 'For all the talk of honour and patriotism', Lyn Macdonald concludes, '... this was a war of greed and territorial ambition'. No less than 28 'principal and associated powers' signed the Treaty of Versailles in 1920, the bulk of them belated belligerents of Germany 'with an eye to advantage and division of the spoils'.[15] Many of them carried promissory notes signed by Britain.

# CHAPTER 2

# The Return to Normalcy, 1918–29

It will be apparent from the preceding discussion that any analysis of British imperialism, in the period under review, involves its shifting relationships with the other imperialist powers as well as its policies towards the dependent territories under its control. This is as obvious in relation to the peace stettlement and its aftermath as it is in connection with the war. The victorious powers assembled at Versailles were intent on punishing Germany, containing – if not eliminating – the Bolshevik virus and securing a new balance of power, a question which automatically included the fate of subject peoples.

The cost to Britain of total victory over Imperial Germany could not be immediately apparent; any final balance sheet had to include much more than the direct economic consequences of the war, and even these were not self-evident in 1918. But it is fair to say that within a few years of the armistice it was obvious that Britain had been gravely weakened, in both economic and military terms, vis-a-vis the United States. It was also apparent that the British Empire was faced with problems that would not go away after the customary show of force. Colonial nationalism survived the repressive measures taken against it in 1919–21. So did Bolshevism, which posed a threat both within and beyond the Empire. At home there was the contradiction of recession and democracy to contend with and an awareness within the political class of its diminished authority. Faced with all of this, the yearning of politicians for a return to the 'normalcy' of 1913 might seem understandable enough, even allowing for the tendency to romanticise the pre-war years. But it was utterly far-fetched as a programme of practical politics. Normalcy, when it came down to it, was understood as British ascendancy in a multilateral, global trading system and returning to this would mean overcoming the insuperable obstacles outlined above.

Britain had been the financial and commercial centre of the capitalist world economy. This dominance had been based, for most of the previous century, on its premier industrial and trading position coupled with its ability to maintain a navy stronger than its next two rivals combined. A vast overseas empire had been accumulated in the course of its commercial expansion, sometimes to secure strategic positions or specific resources, sometimes on the independent intiative of traders, at other times so that the British state could pre-empt a rival. The pattern that emerged was the maintenance under British protection of a vast free trade area. Since so much trade was under British auspices, the international monetary system came to be based on sterling and the centre of the international trade system was located in the City of London, which provided the banking and insurance services that the world economy required. The centrality of London to the global economy allowed Britain to earn more than enough from 'invisible' exports such as shipping services to cover the deficit on its balance of trade.

There was reason to question the long-term viability and utility to Britain of this system from the 1880s, as we have seen. The principal cause for concern was Britain's relative decline as Germany and the United States surpassed its manufacturing output behind walls of tariff protection. Here were states with far greater domestic resources than Britain that could be expected to challenge its international hegemony. Up to 1914, however, Britain retained its naval supremacy, a far superior merchant marine, a global network of military bases and client states, and a clear financial hegemony of the capitalist world, with by far the greatest amount of overseas investment (about £4,000m).

Free trade imperialism thus continued to work for Britain, though there were those such as Joseph Chamberlain who believed that its world leadership could only withstand the challenge of Germany and the United States if it abandoned its cosmopolitan policy and turned to a more systematic exploitation of Empire behind barriers of imperial protection. We will have occasion later on to examine the history of imperial federation. It is sufficient for now to say that the proponents of a closed, imperial bloc were defeated in the general election of 1906. Eight years later Britain entered into a struggle for supremacy against Germany rather than the United States, but when the war ended, the United States was its real victor. It was transformed into the world's greatest creditor nation and all the Allied Powers were indebted to it. Britain emerged from the conflict owing over $1b to the United States, running a growing trade deficit with it, and having lost markets in Latin America to its rival. Britain's direct tax burden was massive by pre-war standards (at around 30 per cent of income) and yet war revenues only met 20.3 per cent of the cost of fighting. The rest came from borrowing and, to a lesser extent, the liquidation of overseas assets. The national debt grew eleven times over. The exchange rate could only be protected by high interest rates, by the transfer of gold to the United States, and by the sale of dollar securities. Government expenditure had risen from 12 per cent of gross national product in 1914 to 51.7 per cent in 1918. A permanent shift in the locus of global financial power from London to New York was now at the least a distinct possibility.

The economic problem was much bigger than this particular balance sheet would suggest, however. The war had dislocated many economies. In most of Europe, prices at the end of the war were two to three times higher than in 1913. Famine threatened most of Central and Eastern Europe. By 1921 total casualties for the period begun in 1914 exceeded 60 million. But at no point did governments consider a coordinated plan for reconstruction. Political considerations obstructed the way. In Britain the 'Coupon' election of December 1918 was actually conducted in an 'atmosphere of vindictive chauvinism'.[1]

It returned the Tory-dominated wartime coalition led by David Lloyd George. But if this was a final spasm of patriotism, the turnout at 57 per cent – the lowest of the century for a British general election – revealed widespread disaffection too. (The even lower turnout of service voters certainly suggests such an interpretation.) What is certain is that well before the end of the next decade the Great War was popularly remembered as an unmitigated, if inexplicable, disaster. Virtually every household in the land had been touched by the casualties. It is hardly surprising that people wished to avoid a repetition of the experience and hoped that the League of Nations embodied new principles of international conduct that made war a thing of the past. The reality was that the peace treaty which created the League was based on the very principles that had caused the war in the first place.

The Treaty of Versailles was signed on 28 June 1919, though the general peace settlement took another five years to conclude. It was almost immediately denounced by the economist John Maynard Keynes, who had participated in the Peace Conference in an official capacity. 'Passion and greed' had prevailed, in Keynes' view, to the point of blinding the victors to their own long-term interests. Germany was to be the victim of a Carthaginian settlement that endangered the industrial future of Europe. The final reparations bill, thanks to demands made by Britain as well as France,[2] lived up to Keynes' expectations. But the signs 'of the fearful convulsions of a dying civilisation' which Keynes saw in 1919, the 'very good' prospects for revolution, were consequences of the war, not the peace settlement. Keynes was right, however, to see that both originated in 'the projects and politics of militarism and imperialism, of racial and cultural rivalries, of monopolies, restrictions and exclusion'. He saw that the treaty was preoccupied with 'frontiers and nationalities ... the balance of power ... [and] ... imperial aggrandisements' as well as 'the future enfeeblement of a strong and dangerous enemy'. President Woodrow Wilson had merely provided

'the web of sophistry and Jesuitical exegesis' which sought to
conceal all this behind high-sounding phrases.[3]

For the duration of the war there had been no public discussion
of war aims, unless one counts the efforts of small groups such as
the Union of Democratic Control and the British Socialist Party.
Governments had sought 'total victory' based on the enemy's
exclusive war-guilt and the political balance had been so shifted to
the right that most socialists subscribed to the official doctrine of
military self-defence.[4] The Bolshevik Revolution of October 1917
profoundly disturbed this consensus, not least because Lenin
immediately exposed the imperialist war aims of all the protagonists.
It was of some importance, then, that President Wilson – who said
that he wanted to 'save democracy' when the United States entered
the war in April 1917 – became the champion of idealistic war aims
from January 1918 when he fashioned his famous 'Fourteen Points'.
Wilson talked, for example, of the 'free and open-minded and
absolutely impartial adjustment of all colonial claims'; the Bolsheviks,
meanwhile, claimed that they had rejected imperialism in deeds as
well as words. But those socialists and liberals who had supported
the war – the vast majority – clearly had a vested interest in believing
Wilson, who offered them an honourable peace and hence a
meaning for the sacrifices of the last four years. In this sense Wilson
'persuaded [them] to acquiesce for over a year in a relatively
unfavourable political status quo for the sake of a supposedly
world-transforming peace',[5] but he did not have to try very hard.

Meanwhile the British and French conducted themselves as if
it was imperialist 'business as usual'. They acted, moreover, as if
most of the colonial peoples were deaf, dumb and blind. The
British Empire delegates, for example, moved to prevent the
Covenant of the League of Nations containing a declaration of racial
equality. But in the colonial world the Wilsonian rhetoric was
taken seriously. The very idea of self-determination obviously
questioned the legitimacy of imperialism. Onlookers wanted to see
how the 'free and open-minded and absolutely impartial adjustment
of all colonial claims' would work out in practice. But nationalists
only had to make the comparison to see that British policy stood
in flat contradiction to the principles of democracy and self-
determination enunciated by President Wilson. The British ruling
class's desire for a return to 'normalcy' involved it in denying
this fact.

Yet nationalist elites had been in evidence long enough to be taken
into account. In India, Ireland, Egypt, Indonesia and China in
particular, the deliberations of the politicians at Versailles were
watched with interest. The nationalists were generally debarred from
the proceedings but during the war promises – both vague and
specific – had been made to some of them along the lines of self-

determination. As it became apparent that the promises would not
be redeemed, so also did it become obvious that the aspirations of
some colonial peoples had grown bolder in the wake of the war and
the Bolshevik Revolution that it helped to provoke. Mass stirrings
against colonialism sprang to life in India, Indonesia and China.
A general crisis of imperialism was beginning and it was in this
context that Britain's last major imperial expansion took place. In
the immediate situation it meant that the return to normalcy would
require substantial repression of nationalists in both India and the
Middle East.

The crisis was already visible to the Viceroy of India in 1917. In
July the British government reluctantly allowed Edwin Montagu,
the Secretary of State for India, to make a statement of Britain's
desire to develop self-governing institutions. It was the first time
any such avowal had been made and it appalled many of Montagu's
colleagues and provoked their often anti-Semitic abuse. Just over
a year later the Montagu–Chelmsford Report was published with
its ingenious proposals for 'dyarchy' – a small measure of provincial
self-government for the 4 per cent of Indians eligible to vote,
combined with continued British control of the centre. Montagu
believed that he had 'kept India quiet for six months at a critical
period of the war'.[6] But almost as soon as the war was over it was
apparent that his constitutional tinkering would not be enough. A
similar problem was evident elsewhere. Egyptian nationalists, after
experiencing the set-back of seeing their country declared a British
protectorate in 1914, were also treated to talk of future self-
government. But the Egyptians were among the peoples that were
locked out of the Peace Conference by the British and prevented
from arguing their case for independence. This snub 'touched off
a widespread national rising, centrally organised and with popular
support'.[7] It was suppressed, of course, but out of the suppression
the Wafd nationalist party was born.

Expediency was at the root of other promises made by the
British. In October 1915, the Egyptian High Commissioner, Sir
Henry MacMahon, talked of how Britain would 'recognise and
support the independence of the Arabs' in return for their help against
Turkey. Six months later the British secretly agreed with the French
to partition the old Ottoman Empire in accordance with the
provisions of the Sykes–Picot Treaty of April 1916. In the eyes of
the strategists, a bigger British presence in the Middle East was
required to check the Russians, now that they had been promised
the Straits and Constantinople.[8] This did not prevent the formulation
of further British assurances of future Arab self-determination,
even though the territories the Arabs had in mind – such as Syria
and Palestine – were the very ones which Sykes–Picot had carved
up for the British and French. And of course when the Bolshevik

Revolution came, and incidentally freed the British and French from their obligations to the Tsar, the Sykes–Picot arrangement survived – it was now said to be required as a check to Bolshevism.

Lloyd George also saw the utility of these Middle Eastern possessions as possible bargaining counters when the time came. This quintessential opportunist was surrounded by ardent imperialists, in both his 'garden suburb' retinue and the Imperial War Cabinet, who could more than match his cynicism with their own enthusiasm for imperial expansion. The Middle East was thought to be rich in oil, a commodity already under British control in Persia and essential for the Royal Navy. Britain's interest in this resource can be traced back to the findings of an Admiralty committee of 1903 and the navy's subsequent turn to liquid fuel in 1912. In 1914 the British government became the major shareholder in the Anglo-Persian Oil Company, with a power of veto over its policy – such was its strategic importance. It was was a measure of Britain's determination to escape the prevailing American and Dutch control of world oil production that the Cabinet took such an initiative. There was thus never much chance of British restraint at the Peace Conference in respect of the Middle East; the war had simply made Lloyd George's government incontinent in its promises. Hence while Arab leaders were assured, behind the scenes, of future independence, the Balfour Declaration of November 1917 promised a national home for the Jewish people in Palestine – one of the territories already spoken for – in the hope that this would prove to be 'useful propaganda' in rallying support for the war among Jews in both Russia and America.[9] Ironically, the day after its announcement Lenin took over in Russia and the various deals to restructure the imperial map were made public.

Anglo-French machinations in the Middle East were conducted in the face of US disapproval. The Americans disliked the secret treaties and Wilson's adviser, Colonel House, publicly denounced them as 'all bad'. The fact that Britain was taking the lion's share could only increase Lloyd George's sense of requiring the goodwill of France – the other major imperialist beneficiary of the settlement – and sharpen his awareness that this set strict limits on how far he could go in moderating French demands for the enfeeblement of Germany. The British and French were thus 'contracturally' bound together, with destructive consequences for both the Middle East and Europe. In the event, Wilson did little to oppose the Middle Eastern carve-up and the United States showed no interest in acquiring mandates of its own in the region. It was content, as it always had been, to dominate its own hemisphere, to which it returned in 'isolation'. It is revealing that the British Cabinet was advised in January 1918 to involve the United States as a trustee in the Middle East on the grounds that Britain lacked the resources to contain the forces of Bolshevism and Muslim nationalism alone. It is even more revealing that nothing came of this prudent advice. Lloyd George saw merit in the proposal – it would also help to answer critics of Britain's own territorial gains – but finally rejected it because 'it would involve placing an absolutely new and crude Power in the middle of all our complicated interests in Egypt, Arabia and Mesopotamia'.[10] In strategic terms the Middle East was of course regarded as a crucial British concern in the defence of the Indian subcontinent, oil or no oil. But Lloyd George's comment is also a reminder of the British political elite's withering contempt for its American counterpart and of the long-lived self-delusion which insisted on the superiority of British diplomacy.

The United States might have been tempted by the mandate for Iraq, already believed to be oil-rich, but the bait was never dangled in front of it; it was evidently thought preferable for Britain to shoulder the whole burden alone than share it with a meddlesome rival. Britain thus acquired what was tantamount to a new empire in the Middle East as Palestine, Transjordan, Iraq and the Gulf states were added to Cyprus, which had been annexed during the war, and the protectorates of Egypt and Aden. The process of imperial expansion in the region was only completed when Britain imposed a treaty on Persia in August 1919. Meanwhile in Africa Britain acquired Tanganyika and parts of other former German colonies, which were added to the Gold Coast and Nigeria; its ally South Africa – led by General Smuts, the man who invented the idea of 'mandates' – secured the mandate for South West Africa.

An additional one million square miles of territory, not to mention 13 million new subjects, was in this way added to the existing 13 million square miles of the British Empire. The formal empire now amounted to one-quarter of the world's land surface and contained the same proportion of the human race – or 450 million people. It contained territories of every shade of dependence, from the self-governing Dominions to the autocratically ruled Crown Colonies, as well as constitutional curiosities such as the Condominium of the Sudan. The various mandated territories, protectorates and nominally independent states of the Middle East which had fallen under British control, linked British India with Egypt and South Africa. One could now travel from Cape Town to Rangoon and never leave the British dominion. No other Power could block the way between Europe and India, or challenge for control of the region's oil and the Suez Canal.

Thus the British Empire grew in spite of numerous warnings of the folly of expansion – a list that must already include Britain's high price for total victory over Germany and the emergence of stiffer resistance to colonialism. Britain had in any case been a satisfied Power in 1914; it had not wanted new territorial acquisitions. War was supposed to be bad for business, especially for Britain – a nation singularly dependent on world trade and already responsible for far-flung possessions not easy to defend. Many of the periodic panics since the 1880s had drawn attention to its national inefficiencies which raised doubts about its capacity to shoulder the imperial burden. In the age of annexations, empire no longer produced benefits without costs – including the costs of defence in a world of rival imperialisms – and it was not obvious that Britain, in relative decline as an industrial power, would be able to meet them. Apart from Germany, there was the American challenge to consider and, far to the East, Japan, already of such concern that something more than a neutralising treaty was concluded with it in 1902 when Britain acquired a new ally. The 'weary Titan, staggering under the too-vast orb of its fate' conjured by Joseph Chamberlain should perhaps have felt utterly exhausted in 1918. But the war was evidently not such a trauma for the decision-making elite that it resolved to keep out of fresh foreign entanglements. On the contrary, it had emerged victorious and with a renewed sense of power.

The narrow stratum of decision-makers was less impressed by the facts of Britain's weaknesses than they were of the apparent strengths in its position. Its main European rival had been defeated and removed from the global game. Germany was deprived of 15 per cent of her arable land, 12 per cent of her livestock, 48 per cent of her iron ore, 15.7 per cent of her coal, 63 per cent of zinc ore, 24 per cent of lead mines and smelting plants, 19 per cent of iron and steel capacity, including 40 per cent of blast furnance equipment. This was before the reparations bill was presented,[11] in which the bond-holding middle classes of Britain had a particular interest; their war certificates would not be devalued if the Germans could be made to pay.[12] Meanwhile German seapower had already been eliminated; the Allies confiscated nearly 90 per cent of her mercantile fleet and the high seas fleet had been scuttled in preference to expropriation. The Rhineland, moreover, was permanently de-militarised.

Britain had crushed its rival. Furthermore, much of Central and Eastern Europe, including Russia, had been plunged into chronic instability, as we have seen. The only power greater than Britain chose to withdraw from the scene when Woodrow Wilson proved unable to obtain Congressional support for his diplomatic initiatives. Britain, with the world's largest navy and air force, had the global imperial field to itself because there was no state of comparable power with the will to interfere. As long as all economic difficulties could be attributed to the war and regarded as temporary, a return to normalcy was thought possible and conceived as a return to the system which the war had disrupted. Yet this focus still involved an inability or refusal to understand the signs that pre-war 'normalcy' was gone forever.

In Ireland, for example, draconian repression following the Easter Rising of 1916 had helped to produce 'a radicalised and insurrectionary movement' against British rule.[13] Sinn Fein had 250,000 members by the autumn of 1917 and went on to win most of the Irish seats in the general election of 1918. But it was still locked out of the Peace Conference in 1919 and the scale of the force required to contain it kept rising until the despatch of as many as 250,000 troops was contemplated. Nor was Ireland the only place where British rule was threatened in 1919. Egyptian nationalists took to demonstrations and violence to protest at their own thwarted self-determination; the British sent more troops and shot demonstrators. In India the year began with country-wide protests against the repressive measures contained in the Rowlatt Bills, which proposed to severely restrict civil liberties as a measure against mounting terrorism. Violent rebellions broke out in many localities including the Punjab. It was here, in the city of Amritsar, that a British officer, General Dyer, gave the order to fire on unarmed demonstrators, killing at least 380 and wounding another 1,200. In the north-west of the subcontinent Britain was involved in the third Afghan war and using aircraft to bomb Kabul. In India's far south-west a rebellion of poor peasants began among the Moplahs of Malabar.

By the summer it seemed that Britain was about to go to war with Turkey again in support of the annexations of Turkish territory approved at Versailles. In Persia it was faced with opposition from nationalists opposed to the treaty which had been imposed in August. In Palestine the problems compounded by Britain's contradictory promises to Arabs and Jews were already apparent before the end of the year, in the first rounds of open conflict between the two communities. It is hardly surprising that by 1920 Sir Henry Wilson, Chief of the Imperial General Staff, was complaining of Britain's military deficit in every theatre with which it was concerned; a year earlier Curzon saw that 'every place is a storm-centre' and his predecessor at the Foreign Office, A.J. Balfour, was worried that Britain's troubles were only just beginning.[14] It was already apparent to the French that the peace established in Europe was merely a 'twenty year truce'. The logic of the settlement with Germany demanded a military alliance of the victors but when American ratification of the treaty was denied by Congress, the burden fell on France and Britain. The British interest, however, lay less in offering guarantees against a German military revival than in blocking the advance of Bolshevism and resuming an imperial role, even though the British delegation at Versailles had contributed more than its share of poison to the European situation with intransigent demands for the greatest possible indemnities. Yet Lloyd George was already daydreaming of a peaceful Germany as a barrier to Bolshevism in January 1919, as the Peace Conference convened to inflict the maximum retribution on it.[15] The reader will not be surprised to learn that he headed a British government 'widely regarded as the most corrupt and irresponsible ... of the twentieth century'.[16]

The economic outlook in Britain offered no cause for optimism about the chances of rectifying any of these problems. The dislocation caused by the war had become even more evident when the restocking boom that began in April 1919 came to an end in the summer of 1920. This proved to be more disruptive than the physical destruction of the war. Excess capacity – already visible in 1914[17] – became an intractable problem for all of Britain's basic industries. In 1921 Britain's industrial production fell by over 18 per cent, foreign trade collapsed by 45 per cent and unemployment rose to 2.4 million or 22 per cent of the insured workforce. It was now that Britain and France presented Germany with a reparations bill of $33b. Elaborate wartime plans for social reform were nevertheless effectively scrapped by the Geddes Committee which recommended extreme cuts in public expenditure in February 1922. By then a deflationary policy designed to cut working-class consumption was in full swing. Less than a year later the German financial system collapsed completely. In Britain itself intensified class conflict, rather than the social harmony envisaged by wartime planners, characterised the decade.

And yet the amount of social expenditure in public spending rose during the inter-war years by two or three times the pre-war level. In part this was obviously because there was no full economic recovery and the costs of unemployment benefit and national insurance weighed heavily on the exchequer. But it was also a cost of democracy and of the associated struggle to contain socialism. At the same time Britain's economic performance relative to the world economy was poor and remained poor throughout the 1920s. Its share of world trade fell from just over 30 per cent of world manufactured exports in 1913 to 20.4 per cent in 1929. Imports rose as a percentage of gross national product and exports never returned to their 1913 absolute levels during the inter-war period. If 1913 is used as a base year (100), British exports stood at only 80.1 by 1924, compared to 107.4 for world exports.

The fact of reduced invisible earnings as a consequence of the contraction of world trade by 1918; the liquidation of overseas investments to finance the war and the consequential weakness of the balance of payments; the huge national febt; the failure of exports in the 1920s – all this meant continuous pressure on the value of sterling. British policy had to find a way round these problems if it was to restore normalcy. Normacly meant sterling restored to its position as the world's principal banker's currency. But for this to happen confidence had to be restored. And for this to take place sterling had to return to the gold standard at the pre-war parity with the dollar, the totem for some – including Churchill, the Chancellor who took the fateful decision in 1925 – of national greatness. If this overvalued the pound – and thus threatened to worsen the balance of payments – another device had to be found to restore the competitiveness of British exports. It was clear to contemporary observers that this device was wage cuts and confrontation with organised labour. But it was also clear that even if this policy was successfully prosecuted, the result would be a further depression of the already depressed demand in the British economy. The determination to reconstruct the pre-war world system was such that this logic was nevertheless pursued relentlessly. In 1925 Churchill accordingly returned Britain to the gold standard at £1 = \$4.86 and sterling was overvalued by at least 10 per cent and the balance of payments was immediately worsened. The stage was set now for a major collision between the British state and the trade unions.

We have already seen that the policy of restoring normalcy made Britain the principal obstacle to colonial nationalism. It also made it leader of the coalition of anti-Bolshevik states. If we go back to 1919 it is clear that all over Europe – and even in Britain itself – the old order was perceived to be threatened by Bolshevism in the minds of the politicians. There was virtual unanimity about this Bolshevik threat at Versailles, controversy revolving only over the best means of eliminating it. Military intervention in Russia in August 1918 had been justified as a measure against Germany, but in practice became an instrument for removing Lenin even before the war was over. Churchill led the faction which strongly favoured all-out war and soon after the Armistice he began to advocate a strong German army to take on the job. By the end of the year some officials were arguing for British protectorates in the Caucasus and trans-Caspia regions where British troops were operating against the Bolsheviks.[18] Lloyd George – rightly conscious of the inflammable industrial situation in Britain – argued that this was the best way to strengthen Lenin in Russia and stimulate Bolshevism at home.[19] Curzon, the Foreign Secretary, was worried that the consolidation of Lenin's government would mean the rich oil resources of the Baku region falling into Bolshevik hands and the spread of the Bolshevik power through Central Asia to the borders of the Indian Empire. All this and more would be 'at the mercy of a horde of savages who know no restraint'.[20] In the event, and with mounting evidence of popular dissatisfaction with British meddling in Russian affairs, Churchill, then War Secretary, was forced to supervise the withdrawal of British forces beginning in March 1919.

Throughout 1919, however, the government continued to assist Denikin's forces in the Russian civil war. In that year alone £94m was spent maintaining a British naval force in the Baltic and the Gulf of Finland blockading Russian ports. Two hundred British warships were involved.[21] In July the Cabinet gave legality to this situation when it formally decided that a state of war existed between Britain and Bolshevik Russia. For the British, Bolshevism was an imperial problem as well as a European problem, as the Russians themselves clearly understood. The imperial dimension of the Bolshevik menace was for some Cabinet members by far its most important aspect and the principal cause of their antipathy. Bolshevism was a contagious virus to which the lower orders, home and abroad, were susceptible. It threatened, for example, to further incite Muslim opinion, which was already incensed by Britain's role in the humiliation of Turkey, seat of the Caliphate. Churchill saw evidence of its disturbing influence in Afghanistan, Persia and India. In November 1920 the Foreign Secretary complained in Cabinet that the British Empire was 'exposed without mitigation to the ceaseless and deadly assaults on the part of the Bolshevik Government and its agents'.[22] But by this time the majority of the Cabinet knew that the opposition of organised labour at home made a full-scale war against the Bolsheviks out of the question. Lloyd George's greater sensitivity on this score no doubt informed his argument that Bolshevism could best be destroyed by trade and prosperity. It is significant that the opponents of his policy in Cabinet included the Colonial, Foreign, and War Secretaries, as well the First Lord of the Admiralty – men with an overseas brief who worried that Bolshevik chickens were hatching all over the place.

Meanwhile Britain's appetite for imperial expansion had pushed Turkey into an alliance with Lenin's Russia. By the Treaty of Sevres (October 1920), the Allies imposed a punitive settlement on the Turks that was harsh even by the standards set by their treatment of Germany. This sparked a nationalist reaction in Turkey led by Kemal Ataturk and it soon became clear that only war could enforce the treaty by which Greece, a British proxy in the region, occupied the whole of Thrace, Smyrna and parts of Anatolia while Britain took control of the Straits of Constantinople. An inter-Allied force occupied Constantinople in March 1920 to enforce the settlement and pronounce Kemal a rebel. This succeeded in provoking a military confrontation which enabled Kemal to forge an alliance with Russia; but the crisis also exposed the unwillingness of the French to fight to enforce the treaty. By August 1921, the Turkish advance on Constantinople and the

Straits zone brought Kemal's troops on a collision course with British forces. In the event armed conflict was avoided thanks to the conciliatory action of the British military leaders on the spot – much to the chagrin of Lloyd George, Churchill and Lord Birkenhead who led the war party in Cabinet. But it was clear that British policy up to this point had actually strengthened Ataturk, who was now armed by the Bolsheviks, while estranging its erstwhile allies. Lloyd George precipitated his own downfall the following year when he encouraged the Greeks, on whom his policy now depended, to attack Turkish forces in Anatolia. Not only were the Greeks routed, but the Greek inhabitants of Smyrna were massacred by the Turks. It has been described as 'one of the worst man-made catastrophes of the twentieth century'.[23]

The dominant influence on Curzon's policy remained Soviet penetration into Central Asia. Clearly Britain's failure to enforce the Treaty of Sevres and the emergence of a Russo-Turkish alliance had only compounded the problem. In the summer of 1921 an inter-departmental committee on 'The Bolshevik menace to the British Empire' was established. Specific complaints were made to the Soviet government in relation to India, Persia, Turkey and Afghanistan as a result of its work.[24] It was the same story in 1922 and 1923. By June 1926 the Cabinet was unanimous in thinking that a breach of relations would be fully justified in view of what the official minutes called 'the malignant hostility to the British Empire in the Soviet Government, repeatedly announced by its leaders and acted upon in all parts of the world and on every opportunity'.[25] After almost twelve months of further allegations of this sort the Die-hards in Cabinet succeeded in bringing about the breach in relations with Russia that they had always wanted. By the summer of 1927 war was widely expected and in the Soviet Union itself 'a state of nervous tension' was said to prevail.[26] But the Die-hards were the very ones least able to see that what all this signified was the persistence of the Bolshevisk state – against all their hopes and expectations – and the impossibility of any return to the 'normalcy' of 1913.

The decision-makers thus put the British state on a course of conflict with nationalism and Bolshevism overseas and organised labour in Britain itself. The war had ensured, however, that the state could not act for long against any of these unless it secured some measure of popular legitimacy. In 1918 the electorate had been increased from eight million to over 21 million and thus placed on an almost democratic basis. But there was no popular movement against imperialism in Britain and, despite the extension of the franchise, the political elite was in some ways as cocooned from the public as ever before, universal suffrage having been simply grafted on to the old pre-democratic institutional structure of government. Though now required to form an 'elective dictatorship', the actual circumstances of post-war Britain – a divided Liberal Party deprived of Irish Nationalist support in Parliament, challenged by a still-nascent Labour alternative – meant that the Conservative Party enjoyed a virtually unbroken hegemony for the next quarter century. For a variety of reasons which we cannot go into here – but which certainly included fear of socialism – it could count on well over 200 safe seats and at least 38 per cent of the vote at a time when the prevailing three-party system ensured that this was enough to prevent any other party from governing alone,[27] and all this in the absence of democratic checks and balances.

Thus the party that had opposed the extension of the franchise was its chief beneficiary. The party of power was the one with the fewest democratic credentials, the one that had most stridently supported the war and demanded the harshest treatment of Germany, the one containing the most enthusiastic imperialists. Of course it suited the purposes of the Conservatives, when the occasion required it, to govern in coalition with others. In 1918, as we noted above, it was expedient to retain the services of Lloyd George – the man who had 'won the war' and who, if the situation demanded it, could handle the potentially rebellious forces of organised labour. Together the Conservatives and Lloyd Georgeite Liberals held 474 seats in the Parliament elected in 1918, while Labour – anathematised as both pacifist and Bolshevist – secured just 59 and on this impotent basis became the offical Opposition. The joint manifesto of the Tory-dominated alliance 'proclaimed that imperialism would be the coalition's chief objective',[28] but it would have been more accurate to say that this occupied joint first position with the objective of stopping socialism – such was the fear of the Left that then prevailed.

The fear of socialism had numerous sources. All forms of socialism looked revolutionary to the middle class of 1918 at a time when the Labour Party was an unknown quantity and working class loyalty had been strained to the utmost by the war. But the huge impact of Bolshevism in Europe, the collapse of four great empires, memories of the pre-war Labour unrest and the fact that British trade unionism had grown enormously during the war all added to the sense of crisis which kept the coalition partners together until 1922. The salience of imperialism is equally obvious. Convinced social imperialists such as Andrew Bonar Law, Curzon and Milner were prominent members of a government chiefly dependent on Conservative support; the character of this support is indicated by its open sympathy for General Dyer after the Amritsar massacre, its hysterical opposition to the mild constitutional reforms proposed for India by Edwin Montagu and its demands for even sterner measures in Ireland at the time of the Black-and-Tan war. In general, of course, the Conservative Party was home for all the imperialist Die-hards in Britain and those who favoured a 'forward policy' of imperial federation and protectionism. Its membership overlapped with that of the most active imperialist pressure groups. The fact that it was in power continuously between 1918 and 1939, with only short breaks of minority Labour administration in 1924 and 1929–31, obviously raises the question of why these schemes were frustrated.

But before examining this point in more detail, the related issue of Britain's straitened economic condition should be raised in connection with its bloated imperial commitments. There is no doubt that the middle class was not entirely happy, given the unprecedentedly high income tax, with the multiple foreign commitments described above. It is clear, moreover, from what has already been said about the balance of electoral forces that pressure from the middle class counted. As early as 1919 the Cabinet decided that in the interests of economy Britain's defence requirements should be scaled down on the assumption that there would be no major war before 1929. This is often said to be the origin of the 'ten-year rule', or the automatic assumption in any year that defence requirements would be based on the absence of major conflicts for the next decade. In fact defence spending was set to rise because of plans to build a fortified naval base at Singapore and raise to 54 the number of RAF squadrons concerned with the defence of Britain. It is, however, a measure of the real weakness of the British economy that budgetary considerations became uppermost, and the ten-year rule first seriously applied, when Churchill (the general-admiral *manque*) became Chancellor in 1924. It was on his recommendation, furthermore, that the Committee of Imperial Defence decided in June 1928 that for purposes of budgeting the ten-year rule should be assumed in any given year.

By 1924, however, the Treasury was straining every nerve to restore Britain to the gold standard. Churchill's decision for defence economies was also made easier by the relative tranquillity of the last half of the decade. Since the early 1920s, moreover, an optimistic assumption had prevailed – Churchill himself was one of its leading enthusiasts – to the effect that air-power offered a cheap, high-tech solution to imperial policing. This theory had been tested to some extent against the Bolsheviks in 1919 when British bombers dropped gas cannisters during the war of intervention. Churchill also approved of their use in Afghanistan during the same year. By 1920 ministers were so convinced of the efficacy of air-power in imperial policing that 37 of Britain's 40 RAF squadrons were stationed overseas.

It seemed to be cost-effective. Mesopotamia (Iraq) provided an instructive example when the British were forced to reconsider the wisdom of the costly imitation of the Raj, with its own Indian-style centralised administration, which they had established in the country in 1919. Though there were almost 100,000 British and Indian troops in occupation at the end of the year, in the wake of the war, the garrison had to be reinforced when a general revolt errupted in the summer of 1920. Fifteen thousand mustard-gas bombs were moved from Egypt for use against the rebels, twelve months after the RAF had first requested them. The expensive governmental apparatus was soon dismantled and a client regime installed under Feisal, one of the sons of the Hashemite Sharif Hussein, who ruled Arabia under a British franchise. Indirect rule and air-power became the complementary low-cost techniques for holding the country; officials anticipated that the cost of governing Iraq would fall from £30m to £6m. Feisal's brother Abdullah, meanwhile, received a subsidy from Britain of just £180,000 per annum for running Transjordan, also with the assistance of the RAF. The brutality required to keep the British in Iraq was remarked upon by T.E. Lawrence in August 1920 when he complained in a letter to the *Times* that 'our government is worse than the old Turkish system. They kept 14,000 local conscripts embodied, and killed a yearly average of 200 Arabs in maintaining peace. We keep 90,000 men, with aeroplanes, armoured cars, gunboats and armoured trains. We killed about 10,000 Arabs in the rising this summer'.[29]

The British government agreed with this in as much as, as Churchill said, the cost of maintaining such a garrison was 'intolerable to the British taxpayers'. Hence the installation of Feisal in August 1921 – devoid of local roots though he was – and greater reliance on the RAF. It had not gone without notice that just six aeroplanes had brought the decades-old resistance of the Dervishes to an end in Somaliland in 1920.[30] Churchill was sure that this was the way to reduce costs in Iraq and indeed so much reliance was actually put on the RAF that bombing villages became a way of raising taxes in the country and was used throughout the 1920s as a way of keeping control in territories with equally difficult terrain such as the North West Frontier, Egypt and the Sudan.

In Egypt, Britain attempted to contain the country-wide rebellion with which it was faced after the war with a combination of repressive measures and the adoption of an even more indirect method of rule than that imposed on Iraq. In 1922 it unilaterally declared Egypt independent, while retaining control of its strategic and economic interests. The nationalist agitation continued, rightly unimpressed. When Sir Lee Stack, Sirdar of the Egyptian army, was assassinated in 1924, the High Commissioner, General 'Bull' Allenby, unleashed a severe repression against 'independent' Egypt.[31] On this occasion his superiors in London deemed that it had gone too far and Allenby was soon retired. But by this time opposition to British rule in the Middle East had been contained, except in distant corners of the most impassable territories. Britain could do what it liked with its possessions because there was nobody to stop it. As Monroe observes, it was able to reign supreme between 1922 and 1929 almost 'without a vestige of military effort'[32] – financial and military support to local collaborators normally sufficed.

Moral scruple certainly was not allowed to get in the way if money and military 'aid' proved insufficient. Churchill in particular was much taken by the use of chemical warfare; gas had become a 'merciful weapon' which exerted a very great 'moral effect' upon its victims.[33] Though he had talked of its 'hellish' character when Germany used it against British troops, it was not just acceptable but even humane when deployed against 'uncivilised tribes'. He might have generalised further; it was the racially inferior who really counted as beneficiaries of the new dispensation. Chemical warfare was only ever contemplated for use against Arabs, Africans and the Chinese (gas was sent to Shanghai in 1927).Years later Lloyd George made the racial rule explicit when he commented on Britain's contribution to the debate on aerial bombardment at the Disarmament Conference in 1932. The British had joined the chorus against this form of warfare – which, like chemical warfare, was then considered barbaric. But they insisted on the legitimacy of such techniques against colonial peoples. Other countries would have agreed to a ban but, as Lloyd George observed, the British 'insisted on the right to bomb niggers'.[34] In fact air-power was used throughout the inter-war period as and when required (as in the suppression of an Arab revolt in Palestine in 1936 when villages were bombed and suspects were interned or summarily shot).[35]

The record thus far shows that the will to persist as a global imperial power had not faltered in the aftermath of the Great War. Certainly, there were developments which contributed to the long-term undermining of the formal empires, but the instinct in Westminster and Whitehall was to resist their pressure. Nor had the set-backs suffered by imperialist Die-hards cured them of their particular delusions. Considering the great unreality of their aspirations, it is the persistence of the social imperialist vision at the highest levels of the Conservative Party throughout the inter-war years that is remarkable, rather than its lack of practical success. Although tariff protection received a crushing defeat in the 1906 election and the enthusiasm for closer imperial coordination generated during the First World War proved short-lived, the Tories returned to protectionism in the general election of December 1923. They failed to win, in the event, and the first minority Labour government went on to abolish most of the surviving import duties. But it is significant that this normally pragmatic party should return to a policy that had dramatically failed it once before. In practice, during the 1920s the Conservatives were confined to such measures as the promotion of emigration in the Empire Settlement Act of 1922 – thanks to which over 400,000 were to take advantage of assisted passage by the early 1930s – and comparatively half-hearted attempts to address domestic unemployment by making modest amounts of colonial aid available in the Trade Facilities Act 1921 and Commonwealth Development Act 1929. They also restored the duties abolished by Labour in 1924.[36]

The Tory prophets of imperial retrenchment nevertheless had the support of pressure groups representing special interests such as the backbench Empire Industries Association and the British Empire Producers Association. More important, the British economy's shape during the prolonged inter-war crisis became more empire-oriented, in the context of its declining share of world trade. Imports, exports and foreign investments all displayed this trend. It was evidently tempting to think that political measures could hasten the process further to Britain's advantage. Increased trade with the colonies might help in alleviating domestic unemployment, assist the balance of payments and ease the national debt. True believers such as Leo Amery, the Colonial Secretary from 1924 to 1929, certainly thought so. In 1928 he saw that the alternative to greater imperial centralisation was continuing relative decline until the point was reached where Britain's absorption into a European Economic Union became inevitable.[37] But the centralising plan Amery favoured was utterly unrealistic for two principal reasons: it depended on the cooperation of the white Dominions, something that their self-interest, heightened by their costly experience of the First World War, precluded; and it involved massive economic development of Britain's black African colonies, something for which Britain lacked the capital even if the City had been willing to pour money into tropical Africa, which it was not.[38] For both reasons social imperialism of the Chamberlain–Amery type was not a practical policy option. Its failure should be seen in this light and not as evidence of the political and economic preponderance of the City and the corresponding weakness of British manufacturing industry, its putative, pro-Empire-bloc rival in such accounts. The political elite certainly regarded the Empire as an asset and was tantalised by the prospect of its systematic exploitation, but was thwarted by the paradox that a position of enormous economic strength was the only basis for turning the Empire into a panacea for national decline.

Of course there were real interests which the defence of Empire was supposed to maintain and the politically significant forces were wholly dominated by those who equated the national interest with its preservation, many of them with a vested interest of their own. Those within the political parties who concerned themselves much with Empire were divided between a majority who talked of Britain's responsibility to care for backward peoples and to act as trustee of their interests, within a framework of free trade and *laissez-faire*, and a minority that stressed the need for imperial development and federation as a means of strengthening Britain. The ruling doctrine in the inter-war period – cognisant as those in power were of the need for an imperialist rationale in accord with 'trusteeship' – asserted the mutual benefit of metropolitan and colonial interests through the operation of the 'dual mandate'. This alleged balance between 'progress' and the protection of local peoples ('native paramountcy', in the jargon of the time) was elaborated at length in 1922 by Sir Frederick Lugard, Britain's permanent representative on the Mandates Commission of the League of Nations. It was a doctrine enthusiastically embraced by successive governments in the inter-war years.

Much of Lugard's argument consisted of the stock-in-trade clichés of late Victorian imperialism. Thus, 'Europe is in Africa for the mutual benefit of her own industrial classes and of the native races in their progress to a higher plane'. British rule, established because of 'the genius of our race to colonise', had unquestionably 'promoted the happiness and welfare of the primitive races'. Just as Roman imperialism had brought the foundations of civilisation to Britain, 'so in Africa today we are repaying the debt, and bringing the dark places of the earth, the abode of barbarism and cruelty, the torch of culture and progress while ministering to the material needs of our own civilisation'.[39] The civilising mission, the social Darwinism, the superiority complex of Lugard's class (masquerading as the 'genius of our race'), the perception of Africa as an 'abode of barbarism and cruelty' – it is all there.

But Lugard's claim to originality rested on his advocacy of 'indirect rule', an idea born of British experience in India but refined during Lugard's governorship of Nigeria, a notably massive and culturally diverse Crown Colony where it was expedient to govern through local collaborators. In India a tiny British presence – the census of 1931 showed just 60,000 in the army, 12,000 in the employ of civilian government – was normally found sufficient, even in the politically turbulent inter-war years. Many things obstructed the emergence of a unified anti-British movement of course, but prominent among them were the Indian princes and their states which comprised two-fifths of the country. Lord Salisbury expressed the hope as early as 1876, in a letter to Disraeli, that the cultivation of this 'aristocracy' might 'serve to hide from the eyes of our own people and perhaps of the growing literary class in India, the nakedness of the sword upon which we really rely'.

Lugard found that the emirates of northern Nigeria could, like the Indian princes, slot into the imperial chain of command. He used his influence to promote this form of rule in the rest of British Africa. Conveniently large, centralised tribal structures with codified customs and laws were not always available, however. In practice indirect rule sometimes meant having to invent the entire apparatus, often enough with disastrous long-term consequences for the societies in question.[40] But with or without social engineering on this scale, indirect rule meant reliance on local reactionaries – a fact that should be set against the claim that the purpose of British rule was the social, economic and political progress of the indigenes.

British experience in the Middle East is a case in point because the relatively low cost of the operation was always an important consideration. Much of the rationale for British occupation was based on the perceived need to defend India. Granted, this was a ludicrous enough argument, but the essential point is that the economic development of the region was never a priority, notwithstanding exploitation of the oil reserves – a wholly different matter. The reactionary character of the local collaborators was thus never an impediment to British objectives and the preferred arrangement was the trade and defence treaty – like the one imposed on Persia in August 1919 – which was concluded with a willing stooge open to friendly advice and annual loans (Curzon advanced Ahmad Shah £2m in 1919, plus the inevitable military equipment and advice). It could then be safely assumed that the client regime had the same interest as the British in so manipulating local divisions among the inhabitants that they never constituted a threat to stability. The retardation of economic life played a notable role in these calculations. As we have mentioned, the Hashemites were adopted for these purposes in Iraq, Transjordan and Saudi Arabia. When Ibn Saud drove them into exile from Arabia in 1925, the British soon started to sponsor the new 'Saudi' regime. The subsidy was designed to purchase the tranquillity of the tribes by furnishing the collaborating party with money and arms – a technique later perfected by the United States in the region. Naturally, this arrangement bought rights to the exploration and exploitation of oil, as in the Persian case where the Abadan refinery, its oil fields, and those of Iraq fell under British control. The same fate befell the oil fields of the Persian Gulf emirates, Yemen and Aden, though the constitutional status of these states varied from one to the other. Iraq remained a puppet of Britain's beyond its independence in 1930, thanks to the enthusiasm of its payrolled monarch.

Obviously the men who appreciated the British best of all in the Middle East were the kings, sultans, emirs, sheikhs and others of landed leisure. These were men 'who feared left-wing ideas' and 'counted on British conservatism to retard the pace of change'.[41] They formed governments of order and obscurantism and steered clear of social reform. Some survived under British protection for a very long time indeed – like the Sultantate of Oman, which was artificially propped up by British subsidies from 1871 to 1970, when the last incumbent was overthrown. As late as 1967 (when oil production began) over half the Sultan's revenue was composed of British money. The local people appear to have received none of it. Even in 1970 their wretched condition is indicated by an infant mortality rate of 75 per cent, illiteracy of 95 per cent, and widespread malnutrition and disease.[42] For the strategists of British imperialism, however, the Sultanate of Oman was a success story, providing an important asset in the defence of the subcontinent and doing so cheaply.

In Britain's African possessions the major wars of subjugation had taken place before the First World War. Reliance on local collaborators now went hand in hand with the exclusion of Africans from important positions in colonial administration.[43] In practice the miniscule number of European rulers, knowing little about the societies they ruled, retained complete control at the centre. 'The basis of European authority was racial. In African colonies whites commanded and Africans obeyed.'[44] Indirect rule made use of the local 'big men' and simultaneously denied the political authenticity of Africans who talked the language of nationalism. The very fact of an educated elite was taken as proof of its severance from any connections with other Africans and of its inability to represent their interests. A 'cruel ideological trap' was thus sprung by European racism in British West Africa.[45] Colonial rule was justified in terms of the backwardness of the colonies and their development by the colonial power. But those Africans who acquired a European education and claimed equal citizenship were debarred from the higher echelons of colonial government on racial grounds, whilst being dismissed as freakish upstarts when they posed as spokesmen of an African point of view.

In the settler colonies of East Africa the white minority sought formal, as well as effective, control of the administrative apparatus. In Southern Rhodesia 'internal self-rule', as it was called, was achieved in 1923. In Kenya the Europeans were less successful but the Hilton Young Commission acknowledged in 1929 that the political influence of the whites had gone far beyond 'the strictly constitutional position'.[46] Indeed, they had also been able to extract assurances from successive secretaries of state regarding the permanent and exclusive nature of white land ownership in the Highlands. It was here that an estate agriculture producing export crops such as sisal and coffee was based, though most settlers relied on the sale of commodities like maize, wheat and dairy produce. Until the Second World War settler agriculture was 'largely a failure',[47] in part because of the incompetence of the Europeans and their 'irrational social aspirations' as Berman calls them – the fact that so many of them expected to live as playboys – as well as the baleful effects of international economic fluctuations. But what developed to sustain Kenya as a 'white man's country' was a far more direct system of rule than anything found in West Africa, made necessary by the need for a ready supply of cheap African labour to service the estates and the demands of the colonial apparatus. Direct and indirect methods of coercion were deployed by the state to produce what one South African observer in the 1920s described as 'probably the cheapest [workforce] in the world', comprising around 220,000 adult males, or 23 per cent of the total.[48]

The economic significance of the African colonies to Britain can be measured in a variety of ways. As export markets they accounted for only 3 per cent of the total of British exports at their inter-war peak in 1938. Between 1907 and 1938 around 85 per cent of the value of exports from sub-Saharan Africa came from the British dependencies. Cain and Hopkins point out that British commercial and financial services 'exercised a near monopoly of colonial business' throughout the period. Thus the chief economic value of these colonies to Britain was in the surplus they generated on visible and invisible trade which made 'a useful, if still modest, contribution to settling Britain's international accounts'.[49] Obviously an array of special interest groups had a stake in emphasising the value of these colonies, including those declining staple industries in Britain that were uncompetitive in other markets and those investors who turned to Empire secure in the knowledge that colonial government loans were supported by an imperial guarantee.

There was a strong perception in political circles, of course, that Britain's own prosperity depended on the markets and products of Empire; Conservatives such as Amery and Churchill believed it, but so did Labour men like J.H. Thomas and Bevin, as well as socialists who opposed the whole system like Orwell and Fenner Brockway. Consciousness of Britain's relative economic decline could serve to highlight the value of maintaining these special relationships. Recently it has been more fashionable to deny that Empire was a source of economic strength, perhaps, as Max Beloff asserts, in reaction to the 'Hobson-Lenin school'. Lord Beloff himself, however, affirms the connection and even suggests that it underpinned political stability in Britain itself.[50] What is not in doubt is that the political class in Britain was persuaded of the connections between British power and prestige, national prosperity and the Empire. An enormous amount of imperialist propaganda took pains to promote these connections in the public mind – the British Empire Exhibition at Wembley in 1924 being an extravagant instance.[51] A wide range of pressure groups agitated in its favour – the British Empire League, the British Empire Union, the Victoria League and the Patriotic League are just a few examples.[52] Nevertheless, as we have noted, the advocates of a more systematic exploitation of Empire were generally frustrated in the inter-war years.

Not the least attraction of 'indirect rule' was that it was cheap. The dependent colonies paid their own way from taxes levied locally. The total British expenditure on the Crown Colonies in 1930, for example, was only £3m.[53] The plans of the social imperialists, by contrast, involved finding large amounts of capital and required a degree of cooperation from the white Dominions which was simply not available. The Imperial War Cabinet, set up in 1917, and the British Empire Delegation to the Paris Peace Conference gave the appearance of unity but the trend was economic divergence and political disharmony. There was no identity of self-interest capable of sustaining proposals for, say, an imperial customs union. The camaraderie and shared institutions which the war created could not long disguise the fact. The Dominions were even reluctant to join the Empire Marketing Scheme established by Amery in 1927. The alliance of the Dominions and Britain was in fact highly conditional, the more so after the war. It was an object of loathing to French Canadians and to virtually the whole of Afrikanerdom and Irish nationalism in any case. The appalling cost of the war, moreover, had weakened the British grip over the hitherto loyal elements. As the Dominions developed their own economies, they in any case developed divergent interests. Britain could no longer act and expect the Dominions to follow, on either economic or diplomatic policy. The British government did not understand this and continued to make much of the necessity of imperial unity in foreign policy. This issue dominated its efforts at the Imperial Conference of 1921. But it was rudely exposed as an illusion when war with Turkey loomed in September 1922 – at the time of the so-called Chanak incident – and Canada and South Africa made clear their determination to refuse automatic military support for Britain.

The creation of the Irish Free State in December 1921 was dramatic evidence of these centrifugal forces, but was not admitted as such at the time. Two years later Lord Curzon was still publicly hankering after a unity that would allow a British Foreign Secretary to speak 'not only for Great Britain alone, but for the whole British Empire ... Think of the addition to his power and strength that will result if, in speaking, he knows – and the world knows – that there lies behind him the sentiments and the might of the British Empire as a whole.'[54] The governing class could never entirely emancipate itself from this chimera of unity. Ramsay MacDonald, the first Labour Prime Minister, sought it in 1924 and the succeeding Tory Foreign Secretary, Austen Chamberlain, simply asserted its existence. The Imperial Conference of 1926 was convened in part to stem the divergent forces which were actually in operation. It is easy to understand why; as Lord Willingdon (Viceroy of India,1931–36) said, possessed of a great imperial federation 'we can snap our fingers at the rest of the world'.[55] For the visionaries of Empire, the thought of Britain at the centre of a huge, self-sufficient economic bloc that was at least the equal of the United States and Russia was too alluring to definitively renounce as impractical.

In fact the British were forced to formally admit in 1926 (in the Balfour Report) what had long been true in practice; the Dominions were sovereign states. Even the settler colony of Southern Rhodesia had secured a limited form of self-government as early as 1921 (in order to safeguard white rule); conflict between the settler colonies and the British government over the future of the black African majority was thereafter a constant problem. Yet, as Barnett observes, the War Office and the Admiralty continued to think as if the military resources of the Empire were at the disposal of Britain.[56] And the next decade began with MacDonald complaining on behalf of the second Labour government, that a British Foreign Secretary could speak with certainty only for the United Kingdom in spite of his having to assume the whole burden of imperial responsibilities. Another Imperial Conference, it was hoped, might promote the desired unity, but by the time it was convened the implementation of the Balfour Report in law (as the Statute of Westminster 1931) turned out to be one of its major preoccupations.

The truth is that the appearance of British security and power which impressed the politicians in 1919 was already threadbare two years later. At home there were serious economic dislocations to grapple with which were soon thought intractable. Abroad Britain was forced to choose, in effect, between American and Japanese imperialism, though both were rivals. America encroached increasingly on British markets and rapidly expanded as a rival naval power. It was engaged in 'a ferocious, though covert, struggle over oil concessions and over cable and radio communications'.[57] Its overseas expansion was the inevitable counterpart of its national economic growth, and this itself was on a continental scale. When Baldwin travelled to New York in October 1922 to negotiate a debt settlement in his capacity as Chancellor of the Exchequer, the real terms of Britain's relationship with the United States became clear – much to the anger of his Cabinet colleagues – when he was forced to accept the conditions of the American banks.

In the Pacific the United States' chief rival was Japan, especially in China. Japan wanted a formal empire in China, while Britain and the United States preferred the 'Open Door', or freedom of exploitation via trade. The irony here is that 'the most distinctive feature of Japanese imperialism is that it originated within the structure of informal empire which the West established in East Asia during the nineteenth-century'.[58] Britain, Imperial Russia and the United States imposed the 'treaty port' system upon Japan, just as they had imposed it upon China. Before the competitive annexations of the 1880s and 1890s, we might say that this was the form of imperialism preferred by the imperial powers. It simply meant that superior force was used to extract privileges by treaty. The weaker country was obliged to accept the unconstrained access to its markets and resources of the imperial 'free trader'. The foreign merchants were to be protected; a foreign garrison might have to be established; a foreign consul too; the subjects of the foreign power were to be tried by consular courts rather than those of the host; the terms of commerce were set by the foreign power; and none of this was to be reciprocated. Such terms were not to be endured by a sovereign state. Japan was long determined to cast them off and then, with the confidence of an emergent power, it had to choose whether its own imperial ambitions in China could be satisfied within the framework of commercial disabilities favoured by Britain and the United States or in opposition to this Open Door system.

We have seen that the British had found merit in friendship with Japan since the alliance of 1902 and that the Great War had underlined its value. Britain had many Far Eastern possessions and already lacked the wherewithal to defend them, given its Atlantic and Mediterranean commitments. But at the Washington Naval Conference, which President Harding convened in 1921, the British were forced in effect to choose friendship with America by dropping Japan. Britain simply could not afford a naval race with the United States, as even the opponents of its appeasement were forced to acknowledge.

In acquiescing in naval parity with the Americans in capital ships, the British admitted at the Washington Conference that the old two-power standard was beyond its means. Economy and *realpolitik* ruled out a war with the United States and this was what really mattered to the British decision-makers, though some of them indulged in the rhetoric of 'Anglo-Saxondom'. Britain's huge national debt, mass unemployment, and outstanding war debts to the United States were a basis for appeasement, not a state of conflict. Thus the alliance with Japan, due for renewal in 1922, was abrogated in deference to American hostility and its fear of a possible Anglo-Japanese military combination. Yet under the terms of the

Washington Conference, Japan was allowed a navy three-fifths the size of Britain's – not big enough to present the Americans with a problem but too big for Britain's over-stretched forces to have to contend with. Britain left the conference, then, faced with a new insecurity in the China Seas and possessed of only formal naval equality with the United States. Yet absolute naval dominance had been trumpeted as a prerequisite of the British Empire for as long as anyone could remember.

Against all the economic indicators, the booming American economy was vastly more powerful than that of the British in the 1920s, though the geographical extent, population and imagined aggregate wealth of the British Empire served to obscure that fact from some observers on both sides of the Atlantic. By the end of the 1920s the United States had replaced Britain as the main trading partner of China and Japan and had displaced Britain as the chief foreign investor in Canada and Latin America. Indeed it supplied two-thirds of all new long-term foreign investment in the decade. Britain was also in retreat in South American markets, accounting for only 16 per cent of the region's imports at the end of the decade against 38 per cent for the United States. For all this there was a widespread conviction in the United States that Britain's Empire gave it unfair competitive advantages such as monopolies of raw materials. In Britain it was understood that American imperialism, the 'American money power' as Baldwin called it in 1929,[59] was determined to break down the imperial barriers.

A case in point was the successful American campaign to counter the burgeoning British oil monopoly in the Middle East, where it controlled production in southern Persia and threatened to do the same in Iraq. It was here that American interests, represented by Turkish Petroleum, secured a share of the concession in 1925. The supply of rubber was another source of contention. Britain already controlled three-quarters of the world output when it decided to cut production in 1922 to 60 per cent of its 1920 total, on the grounds that over-supply was ruining planters in Ceylon and Malaya. The United States, consumer of two-thirds of the world's rubber, chiefly because of the automobile boom, was faced with a price of $1.21 per pound by 1925, compared with just 16.3 cents in 1921. In the ensuing diplomatic squabble the British observed that US raw cotton was subject to exactly the same kind of manipulation. Indeed the British developed alternative imperial sources of supply to break the US stranglehold and the Americans solved their own problem by turning to Dutch Indonesian suppliers who were outside the British cartel. They also used financial blackmail against the ostensibly independent state of Liberia, which was obliged to produce rubber on terms set by the Firestone tyre company.[60] In the event the British were forced to abandon their quotas for rubber production in 1928, by which time they controlled just half of world supply.

Such was the continued uncertainty in Anglo-American relations – the Soviet Union confidently anticipated an imperialist war between the special friends throughout the 1920s – the responsibility for conducting relations with the United States became the personal responsibility of the Prime Minister in the second Labour Government formed in 1929. One of his earliest 'successes' was recorded in June of that year when the British Government finally bowed to the inevitable and accepted parity in cruisers with the United States. Twelve months later it had cause to curse Washington again when Congress adopted classic beggar-my-neighbour policies in the shape of the Smoot-Hawley Tariff and wrecked any hope that collaboration between the two governments could address the economic crisis. By that time the economic collapse precipitated by the Wall Street crash had finally killed the Treaty of Versailles as well as the idea of a return to normalcy.

# CHAPTER 3

# The World Crisis, Appeasement and Imperial Survival, 1929–39

The second minority Labour government, which took office in June 1929, did nothing to disturb the continuity of imperial policy. The party leadership accepted the fact of the British Empire and subscribed to the official ideology of trusteeship. It fashioned no conception of the national interest or of defence strategy that might challenge the idea that British power and prestige in the world depended on the maintenance of Empire. The Labour movement was broad enough to contain critics of British imperialism and some of them served on the party's advisory committee on imperial questions. The gulf between policy and advice was never bigger, however, than on imperial issues. But even the reformers failed to break free of many of the ruling prejudices of the time. Many assumed the permanence of the existing international division of labour, believed that to support free trade was to be anti-imperialist, were quite unconscious of their own racism and uncomprehending of colonial nationalism.[1]

The Independent Labour Party – which seceded from the Labour Party in 1932 – had always taken a more internationalist view and inclined towards a Leninist understanding of international relations during the 1920s. It came out in favour of Indian independence in 1926 and adopted an increasingly uncompromising anti-imperialist stance that was for the most part indistinguishable from that of the Communist Party. Neither of these parties, however, succeeded in making imperial issues prominent within the trade unions or the Labour Party, though their failure was not for want of trying and the communist agitation around the Meerut Conspiracy Trial certainly caused a stir at the highest levels of the labour movement. The communists in particular repeatedly brought colonial issues to the attention of left-wing activists – issues such as the use of forced labour, institutionalised racism, censorship and the repression of trade union and political activity, as in the case of the Meerut defendants.[2] The Labour Party itself, however, did not even campaign against the injustices and abuses exposed by its own liberal humanitarians, let alone take an advanced position on the future of the colonies.[3] Norman Leys, C.R. Buxton and

Leonard Woolf of the party's imperial advisory committee had no discernible impact when they demanded action against the 'colour bar' in East Africa or real international trusteeship of dependencies or genuine steps toward self-government. Nor was the party much ahead of the Conservatives over the future of India. Indeed, by 1929 it was 'disliked as much as the Conservatives in influential sections of Indian political opinion, ranging from the moderates to the radical nationalists or the trade union leaders'.[4]

Ramsay MacDonald had set the tone at the outset of his first government in 1924 when he gravely warned the Indian nationalists that 'no party in Britain will be cowed by threats of force'. The nationalist leaders, it will be remembered, were constitutionalists and moderates to a fault. MacDonald's motive in issuing this superfluous statement is better understood in the light of his choice of ministers for the relevant departments of state. Seasoned imperialists predominated and the message was clear: business as usual. MacDonald was as hostile to nationalist demands as the Conservatives and as much opposed as they were to League of Nations interference in imperial matters. His second government coincided with, and did nothing to obviate, Gandhi's second great civil disobedience campaign which was launched at the beginning of 1930. Nor did it prevent the passage of the Tory-inspired Southern Rhodesian Land Apportionment Act in the same year, which segregated the land rights of Africans and Europeans, giving the latter all the best parts of the country.

There were enthusiastic imperialists in the labour movement who could rival Tories such as Amery and William Ormsby-Gore in their passion for colonial development. The country's persistent economic problems in the 1920s persuaded even some of the party's left-wing – John Wheatley and George Lansbury included – that the answer was empire development 'under a socialist inspiration'.[5] In 1925 20 Labour MPs supported a Conservative motion in favour of imperial preference in the House of Commons. A far larger number belonged to the Labour Commonwealth Group of MPs led by the staunch imperialist, Leslie Haden-Guest. J.H. Thomas, Colonial Secretary in MacDonald's first government, publicly talked in 1925 about the economic development of African resources, combined with the price-fixing of resources such as rubber, as a means of strengthening the pound against the dollar (it was the year of Britain's precarious return to the gold standard). Later in the decade Ernest Bevin, leader of the Transport and General Workers' Union, made a lasting conversion to the creed which linked British prosperity to the development of its colonial resources.[6] In July 1929, Labour actually produced a Colonial Development Act concerned to assist British exports, but it provided just £1m per annum over three years for this purpose. The Labour government was in thrall to the economic orthodoxy of free trade under the gold standard and balanced budgets. Any economic intervention to address the problem of unemployment was accordingly restricted to gestures of this type.

Labour's leaders remained committed to pre-war liberal economics even though the world economic crisis – which began within months of the formation of the government – had destroyed all of its assumptions before it engulfed the government itself. Labour's fidelity to the 'sound money' doctrine is all the more ironic because one of its major attractions for the British Establishment, in fact, had always been its utility in obstructing social expenditure by a Labour government and in disciplining the organised workforce. Indeed this was the logic to which MacDonald himself was eventually driven, though without the wholehearted support of his Cabinet. In August 1931 he resigned the government, only to reappear with his Chancellor Philip Snowden and J.H. Thomas as leaders of a new 'non-party' coalition dominated by the Conservatives. At the end of October this so-called National Government was returned to power on the strength of what was, in effect, the biggest ever Conservative electoral victory. It now proceeded to do what had been impossible for the previous Labour administration. It took Britain off the gold standard in September 1931 and introduced tariff protection.

The breakdown of the liberal international economic order had roots going back to the First World War, as we saw in the last chapter. Britain had survived this conflict at an enormous cost to its role as an international banker. It had emerged with a greatly swollen national debt, the servicing of which absorbed as much as 40 per cent of public expenditure in certain years. With reduced foreign investments it had lost invisible earnings as well as markets for its goods. All this undermined foreign confidence in sterling, particularly as domestic pressure to increase public expenditure had also risen in the wake of total war. The 1920s began, it will be recalled, with one of the worst economic depressions in British history.

Internationally, matters were made worse by the United States' refusal to write off war debts. This in turn made resolution of the German reparations problem more difficult. The American failure to perform Britain's pre-war global role as manager and guarantor of the international system of payments was also signified by its adherence to tariff protection (which was raised to new heights in 1930) even at a time when it recorded huge trade surpluses and held enormous credits. This parochial approach was reflected in the large flow of gold to the United States up to 1924, which put the world – but particularly Britain – under deflationary pressure.[7] The fact that Britain persisted, in the face of all this, to attempt to play the world financial role of the past is of course partly explained by the United States' failure to take a wider view of its interests.

The City of London was determined to restore the pre-war prestige of sterling. It shared the widespread conviction in governing circles that restoration of the gold standard would symbolise a return to the normalcy of 1913. The inflated dollar exchange rate that was actually adopted was intended to signify a return to sterling's 'top currency' status and thus the restoration of Britain's role of world banker, with the City as the premier global financial market. The gold standard was supposed to operate as a self-regulating market beyond political control. In the eyes of the sound money school, this had the additional virtue of enabling the Treasury to control public expenditure and restrict the scope of government economic activity. Naturally this was attractive to the vast majority of industrialists, though there were those such as Sir Alfred Mond of ICI who believed the cost to production and employment was too high.[8]

The upshot of all this was priority for Britain's global commercial and financial role at the expense of both short-term employment and social reform. The fact that all three political parties subscribed to this arrangement says a great deal about the long-standing hegemony of free trade doctrine and the assumed convergence of interests between British industry, and the commercial and financial interests of the City which were thought to flow from it – including, in practice, the maintenance of Britain's overseas territorial possessions. It is true that voices – sometimes industrial voices – had been critical of these arrangements since the 1880s, but let us not forget that in the early 1920s the British Empire had never been bigger and Britain still held the largest share of overseas capital. The trade area using sterling remained the largest trading zone in the world; furthermore, there was no understanding that the pre-war 'normal' had vanished for good. In restoring the gold standard, the Chancellor, Winston Churchill, told the House of Commons in the debate on 4 May 1925 that 'it would be impossible for London to retain its position as the centre of the British Empire and world finance unless it were to march with the movement in the direction of establishing a common foundation for all international transactions ... We were often told that the gold standard would shackle us to the United States. It would shackle us to reality.'[9] Of course it is of some interest that Labour was unable to specify Britain's economic interests in another, equally coherent, way. But then, neither did British industry, even when the benefits of the traditional arrangements began to falter conspicuously, as they did in the 1920s.

In part this was due to inertia; the pre-war arrangements had worked for so long, it was difficult to find a convincing alternative.

The economic and political ramifications of the old system were inextricably connected and difficult to distinguish. The ruling class firmly believed that they had presided over the gradual, providential march of national greatness and they were unlikely to surrender this view of themselves in a hurry. The Empire – a huge outgrowth of this national evolution – was an unfinished project in terms of this Whig theory of history. As Barnett observes, furthermore, 'everybody in the British governing class had a friend or relative who had been in India, was in India, or was going to India'.[10] There were many such personal aspects of the imperial commitment. It was a function of the elite schools, for example, to turn out the administrators of Empire and – such was the scale of the imperial enterprise – there was no shortage of glamour and the appearance of power to attract their pupils into its service. Between 1919 and 1948, indeed, recruitment to the colonial services was left in the hands of one man, Sir Ralph Furse, who looked to the public schools for the appropriate human (and class) material.

The governing party, increasingly plutocratic and commercial though it undoubtedly was, also retained the services of the landed element within the apparatus of empire. This is significant in determining that an important component of the imperial 'inter-governmental lobby' was drawn from the section of the ruling class that was least comfortable with political democracy in Britain, the types who withdrew, more or less self-consciously, to the democracy-free zones of the Empire or the least accountable branches of British government. At home this element was disproportionately present at the Foreign Office, the Colonial Office, the Dominions Office, and the India Office. The War Office and the armed forces were the other domestic sites for this relatively impecunious aristocracy.[11] It is not necessary to collapse the whole explanation of imperialism to an atavistic impulse[12] to see that the influence of such men – more heedless of national economic realities than most, disdainful of the lower orders and passionately convinced of the strategic necessity of every British possession and of their own genius for governing them – could only be baleful.

The exclusive club atmosphere of the Foreign Office – 'the last choice reserve of administration practised as a sport', according to Cannadine – was accordingly congenial to this caste, members of which served in conspicuous numbers both as ministers and full-time officials.[13] 'The broadly recreational character of foreign policy' and the 'politically and intellectually undemanding character of the routine conduct of foreign affairs'[14] helps to explain both the attraction of this kind of work and the ready supply of those with a capacity for it. Schooled to think in grandiloquent terms about the imperial power and its responsibilities, few of these men were encumbered by any great ability or even much knowledge of the places they governed. In virtually ever major embassy and throughout the corps of career diplomats the scions of landed families were to be found in occupation throughout the inter-war years. Sometimes there was even a dynastic element in this grip on diplomacy; at all times there was a carefully preserved social exclusivity and detachment from public opinion. Recruited young, furthermore, the personnel of these branches of the state enjoyed an unusual longevity of career so that those who reached the pinnacle of the Foreign Office in the 1930s, say, were products of the regime prevailing in the 1900s with its attendant reactionary attitudes.[15] Bound together by common values, a strong sense of their own superiority and fitness for wielding power free of the constraints of democratic accountability, these men enjoyed all the conditions of secrecy and permanence of office conducive to arrogance, complacency, hypocrisy and questionable judgement.[16]

'Between the 1880s and the 1930s, the British Empire provided secure, comfortable, well-paid, and essentially ornamental employment opportunities in quite unprecedented numbers. And the result was a system of outdoor relief for the upper classes on a scale of which even John Bright had never dreamed.'[17] Numerous governors, viceroys, and even lesser place-hunters bore this patrician stamp. Even the rulers of British Africa – so much less desirable than India and the Dominions though it was – came to an overwhelming extent from the new urban gentry of southern England.[18] But while the military strategists and holders of imperial sinecures undoubtedly represent a vested interest in the maintenance of Empire, the British state's chief stake in Empire derived from the economic and political power it was supposed to confer on the nation.

The inter-war years provided a mass of contradictory evidence to both support and question this perception. Earnings from both visible and invisible exports shrank in the wake of the war, while imports increased. Britain's share of world manufactured exports fell from 26 per cent in 1913 to 21 per cent in 1929 and 19 per cent in 1937. The pre-war balance of payments surplus was reduced in the 1920s and actually went into deficit between 1934 and 1938. In the 1930s Britain was forced to reduce overseas assets to cover import payments and the rate of this disinvestment amounted to the equivalent of 1 per cent of Britain's gross domestic product per annum.[19] New York had already emerged as an effective rival source of long-term investment in the 1920s, offering more competitive rates than London which was further hampered by Britain's struggle to restore the gold standard. Britain's overseas loans were inevitably lower than the levels achieved in the years 1900–14; they fell even more in the 1930s, in the context of world recession, dropping to levels comparable with those of the early nineteenth century. The evidence afforded by hindsight thus shows a trend of diminishing relative economic power for the nation with the world's largest empire and correspondingly enormous military obligations.

But even if the evidence of Britain's decline had been unequivocal – and we shall soon see that this was not the case – the point of departure for policy-makers was necessarily the pre-war 'normal' which they were determined to restore. Throughout the 1920s their minds were fixed on this. In the memory, India, for example, was a major field of British investment with £800m of its £4b of overseas capital in 1914 tied up on the subcontinent. Certain interests in Britain were particularly dependent on the Indian market (cotton being the best pre-war example), while others made money from its raw materials – its jute mills, for example, continuing to make an annual profit of 90 per cent into the 1920s.[20] Then there was the contribution to imperial defence and regional power of its self-financed army. This had been real enough during the First World War – it amounted to 1.5 million men – but India's might was also symbolic of Britain's Great Power status and entered imperial calculations in a correspondingly sentimental way.

In the pre-war order, India had maintained a trade surplus with the rest of the world by its export of primary produce while running a large deficit with Britain by virtue both of its imports of manufactured goods and the costs of supporting the government of India. British control of this market on the eve of the war is indicated by its supply of 80 per cent of these imports compared to only 8.5 per cent from Germany.[21] Ingham points out that India's overseas earnings had been deliberately used to cushion the impact of sterling crises and ease the City's own liquidity problems.[22] India was also kept on a silver standard throughout the nineteenth century so that gold could be drained from the country; indeed the gold drain continued into the 1930s with around £241m worth leaving the country for Britain in the years 1931–37.[23]

Following the economic dislocation caused by the war, India's value as an export market for British manufactured goods was greatly reduced. Indeed the Indian Industrial Commission, appointed in 1916, had recommended the rapid industrialisation of the subcontinent as a device that would bring a great access of strength to British power. Obviously the war emergency was the proximate cause of this reversal of British policy and once the crisis had passed so did the sense of urgency that had inspired the change. The development of import-substituting manufactures which the war stimulated in India nevertheless continued at a slower pace in the 1920s and British policy – mindful of nationalist business opinion and of the need for balanced budgets – actually raised the general tariff on Indian imports in 1921 and 1931. The combined effect of India's own manufacturing growth, the penetration of the Indian market by Britain's industrial rivals, and the British government's tariff policy was enough to squeeze British exports severely, particularly cotton textiles. Whereas two-thirds of India's imports in 1914 had been supplied by Britain, by the 1930s its share was down to one-third, while the combined share of Japan, Germany and the United States had risen from about 10 per cent in 1914 to over 33 per cent by 1936. At the same time Britain took a growing proportion of Indian exports, indeed one-third of their total by 1938–39. India also attracted only a small increase in British investments during the inter-war years.

It remained, however, one of the single biggest sites of British investment and a useful tool of British economic policy. The same 'sound money' doctrine which prevailed in Britain was imposed on India, helping Britain to restore itself to the gold standard in 1925 and continuing to supply the metropolis with gold thereafter. In the 1920s India was thus 'drawn into Britain's efforts to reconstruct the pre-war international economic order; and in the 1930s ... [it] was ordered into the sterling bloc on terms dictated by London'.[24] Furthermore, 'remittances from the subcontinent accounted for 15–16 per cent of Britain's total net invisible earnings in the 1930s and made a vital contribution to the stability of sterling and the balance of payments at a particularly difficult time'.[25] Even as a market India remained important to Britain; though its share of this market contracted, visible exports to India still represented 9 per cent of the total of British exports in the 1930s (as compared with 13 per cent in 1913). British multinationals, moreover, figured prominently in the development of import-substituting manufactures in India itself.

The overseas expansion of British corporations was already significant before the First World War but it experienced a marked spurt of further growth in the 1930s, when circumstances made the Empire the obvious direction to take. The great merger boom of the 1920s helped to pave the way, though Empire had already enabled firms such as Dunlop and Imperial Tobacco to achieve a position of dominance in certain colonial economies; the formation of cartels and combines also facilitated their control of the most valuable colonial resources. ICI, Unilever, EMI, Tate and Lyle, Cadbury-Fry, Amalgamated Press and Courtaulds were leaders among the firms establishing a network of subsidiaries within the Empire during the inter-war years. Unilever, for example, formed the conglomerate United Africa Company in 1929 from the merger of 37 companies; by 1936 it controlled 56 per cent of Nigerian exports of palm-oil, cocoa and peanuts.[26] As Hannah points out in relation to another product of the merger boom:

the title Imperial Chemical Industries was ... no accident, for, as the founders said:

> The British Empire is the greatest single economic unit in the world ... By linking the title of the new company to that unit, it is intended to lay emphasis upon the fact that the promotion of imperial trading interests will command the special consideration and thought of those who will be responsible for directing this new company ... and it will be the avowed intention of the new Company, without limiting its activities in foreign overseas markets, specially to extend the development and importance of the Chemical Industry throughout the Empire.[27]

The economic significance of Empire, as this statement suggests, grew in perception as well as in fact, during the inter-war period. While British trade declined as a proportion of world trade, imperial trade represented a growing proportion of the total. Colonial imports rose from 25 per cent of British imports in 1910–14, to 31 per cent in 1930–34 and 40 per cent in 1939. Exports to the colonies likewise contributed a growing fraction of the total: from 36 per cent in 1910–14 to nearly 50 per cent in 1939. Britain was overly dependent on labour-intensive, staple industries which British financial policy had rendered even less competitive in world markets by returning the country to an inflated parity with the dollar in 1925. Given these constraints, imperial markets had been a relatively soft option since 1918 – though even a soft option could not always compensate for the ineptitude of British manufacturers (who failed to make the most of markets such as Malaya). With the collapse of the gold standard in 1931 the economic significance of the Empire grew stronger nonetheless. This was also true for the City. Though the amount of overseas investment had still not returned to the 1914 level, the share of British foreign investments going to the Empire increased. Thus what was true for British exports was now also true for British finance as the quest for liberal cosmopolitanism was finally abandoned and the City reconciled itself to the reality of protectionism. The perceived link between British economic power and the preservation of Empire was inclined to grow under these circumstances.

Henceforward Britain successfully shielded itself against the worst effects of the world slump by organising a sterling bloc centred on Empire. The general response to the breakdown of the international economy after October 1929 reinforced protectionist and imperialist tendencies everywhere. Political and military power, cartels and exclusions,[28] once more became attractive instruments of economic advancement in the absence of any possibility of a return, under the protection of a hegemonic power, to a liberal world system. Not that the 1920s had been trouble-free; the prevailing political disorder is indicated by the fact that to patch up the business left unresolved by Versailles no less than 23 international conferences had been convened between 1919 and 1922. On the economic front the United States had pursued beggar-my-neighbour policies well before the Wall Street crash and weaker states had inevitably followed the same course of action. By 1927, for example, the average *ad valorem* tariff on manufactured goods was already 20 per cent in Germany, 21 per cent in France and 34 per cent in the United States. Nevertheless, the world economic crisis greatly deepened the trend, with the United States leading the way through the Smoot-Hawley Tariff Act of 1930. The collapse in the American stock market which precipitated the crisis devastated metropolitan farming and business interests everywhere from France to Japan. It strengthened the hand of those who promised national salvation from slump and socialism by means of overseas expansion and authoritarianism. The collapse of world trade led directly, for example, to the Japanese occupation of Manchuria in 1931.[29] The following year a massive upsurge of support was recorded in both the Presidential and Reichstag elections for the Nazis in Germany, where unemployment stood at around 30 per cent. Here the world economic crisis 'was first and foremost a political event' signifying 'the collapse of a political experiment' – the Weimar Republic.[30]

It was at this late stage in the crisis that Britain withdrew from the gold standard and devalued sterling. A year earlier the financial institutions of the City of London had publicly acknowledged the death of free trade and the Federation of British Industries revealed that 96 per cent of its members voting on the issue favoured tariffs.[31] The Beaverbrook and Rothermere press had waged a concerted campaign for protection under the slogan 'Empire Free Trade' since 1929. This in itself reflected the existence of a body of disaffected opinion including that of businesses such as ICI, British Small Arms, and British American Tobacco. But it also overlapped with the campaign to remove Baldwin from the leadership of the Conservative Party on the grounds of his alleged retreat before the independence movement in India. The press barons used all eight of their national newspapers in this crusade for a forward imperial policy but overreached themselves by launching a new party in February 1930, the United Empire Party, which threatened to divide the ruling class and destroy the power of the Conservative Party. For this *faux pas* Beaverbrook was pronounced a 'mad dog' by Lord Hailsham and advised by the banker, Sir Henry Strakosch, that 'it is more important than ever to avoid any internecine strife amongst those who believe in the maintenance of the established order'.[32] A month later Beaverbrook found a compromise with the Conservative Party in the so-called Stornoway Pact which he negotiated with Neville Chamberlain in March 1931; Baldwin agreed to employ quotas, prohibitions and duties to help agriculture and Beaverbrook agreed, in return, to end his 'crusade'.

In February 1932 the National Government imposed a general tariff of 10 per cent *ad valorem*, exempting the Crown Colonies. In July and August, at the Ottawa Conference, a system of imperial preference was agreed between Britain and the Dominions. The day of 'Empire Economic Unity had dawned' according to Beaverbrook.[33] The only trouble was that it had not. The British had initially wanted Empire free trade but the Dominions refused to lower their tariffs to any significant degree and the outcome was a system of trading preferences that were actually more generous on the British side. This seems to be borne out by the trade figures which show that exports to the Dominions averaged £143m in 1925–29 but fell to £111m in 1934–38, or by 22 per cent. The overall fall in export values, however, was 38 per cent in the same years as world trade contracted. But the question remains why did Britain concede better terms for Dominions' exports than they did for Britain's, with the result that the concessions agreed at Ottawa helped increase Britain's exports by only 5 per cent by 1937 while imports from these parts of the Empire rose 10 per cent?[34]

In part the British miscalculated, not for the first time, the degree of complementarity of the Dominion and metropolitan economies. The Dominions' own manufacturing lobbies, persistent balance of payments problems and inability to borrow from Britain – whose overseas investments were by now tiny compared to the scale of debt repayments – all operated against imported manufactures and in favour of domestic alternatives. In short the Dominions would not endanger their own manufacturing industries – a point which imperialists like Beaverbrook refused to understand even though it had been spelled out at the Imperial Conference in 1930 by the Canadian Conservative Prime Minister, R.B. Bennett, who declared Empire free trade to be 'neither desirable nor possible'. At Ottawa, then, concessions over tariffs were a price the British had to pay to get any sort of agreement. But they may also have been a price worth paying for Britain's continued financial authority in the world.[35] For it was at this point – from the collapse of the gold standard – that the sterling area was born comprising those countries, like the Dominions, that were heavily dependent on British trade. Such countries – they included all Empire countries except Canada and British Honduras, as well as some that were outside the Empire – did most of their trade and held most, if not all, of their reserves in sterling and fixed their currencies in relation to the pound.

We will see in the next two chapters that the sterling area played an important economic role for Britain and allowed the pound to survive as a major banker's currency. In the 1930s Britain's net trade deficit with the Dominions caused no problems for the value of the pound because it increased the sterling balances which the Dominions held in London. This in turn allowed these countries to meet their sterling obligations without recourse to borrowing or by posing the threat of default. As dependents on British credits, British financial services and shipping, the Dominions had plenty of obligations to meet. 'Default or repudiation could have destabilised sterling and might even have led to the collapse of the sterling bloc.'[36] Preferential treatment in the British market thus served Britain's wider purpose and substituted for its inability to lend in the 1930s.

The sterling area thus seems to have played its part in enabling Britain to weather the world crisis. London retained its global financial role and Britain retained its share of world trade. Tariff protection helped in cushioning the British economy from the worst effects of the global contraction in trade. One detailed study of the effects of protection has found that export competitiveness improved by 2.5 per cent in 1931–37, relative to 1929, and import competitiveness by 5.4 per cent.[37] But this was in the context of a chronic slump in the world economy. Britain's fundamental economic problem – over-commitment to the technologically backward basic industries and an inability to replace them with internationally competitive new industries – persisted as a cause of weakness. Chronic balance of payments deficits were all the worse for occurring at a time when British decision-makers were conscious of the Empire's strategic overstretch in the face of Japanese expansionism in Asia and fascist aggression in Europe and Africa.

This consciousness of weakness was the basis for the appeasement of the fascist powers. Appeasement itself was no new thing in the obvious sense that British policy had always tried to avoid involvement in a major European war. Since 1918, however, the gap between Britain's global interests and its ability to protect them had grown larger. The British Empire was often depicted as a vast arrangement for collective security – certainly so far as its white components were concerned – but in truth it lacked the means to give substance to this aspiration. But while Conservative politicians might consider buying off aggressors such as Nazi Germany with colonies between 1935 and 1939, there was no suggestion of imperial retreat. Chamberlain had in mind other people's colonies, specifically Portugal's and Belgium's in Africa. It is an episode which demonstrates just how much colonies were thought to matter; they certainly did for the British governing elite which persisted with its colonial bait in the face of all the evidence that Hitler was not interested.[38] But there was no scaling-down of Britain's own imperial commitments in the inter-war years; any suggestion that American naval power was required to protect Australia and New Zealand, for example, was dismissed out of hand.

Appeasement nevertheless entered the picture here in the sense that
the British were forced to look for ways of retaining the Empire in
the face of growing discontent within it and in the knowledge that
they lacked the option of overwhelming force.

In India constitutional reform had been a response to demands
for self-government – and an attempt to defeat such agitation – since
the Indian Councils Act of 1909. The Montagu Declaration of 20
August 1917 was the first to refer to 'the gradual development of
self-governing institutions' in India but its authors – including the
Die-hards Lord Curzon and Austen Chamberlain – did not envisage
Indian independence. Indeed, though the Declaration implied a
future Dominion status, even a decade later it was not clear whether
the time required to get there was measurable on anything less than
geological calendars. The Montagu–Chelmsford Report (1918)
recommended the system of 'dyarchy' that was introduced in the
Government of India Act of 1919. It was an attempt to widen the
Raj's base of support. By enfranchising 4 per cent of the population
and allowing them to elect provincial legislatures with a limited
degree of autonomy, it was hoped that the moderates would be co-
opted into British rule. The Viceroy retained autocratic powers and
the appearance of the Rowlatt Act, General Dyer and martial law
in the Punjab during the same year were reminders that the British
had by no means dispensed with coercion.

In 1924 the Labour government offered the same combination
of constitutionalism and coercion; MacDonald asked for faith in
British democracy and future constitutional advances while dealing
with disaffection with practical measures like the Bengal Emergency
Ordinances, which allowed imprisonment without trial. But it was
the Conservative Die-hard, Lord Birkenhead, who began another
long round of constitutional charades in 1927 when he created the
Simon Commission to enquire into the workings of the Act of 1919.
This body enraged political India for failing to possess a single Indian
representative (which did not prevent C.R. Attlee from participating
on behalf of the Labour Party) and provoked riots and boycotts
wherever it travelled on the subcontinent in 1928 and 1929.
Though Motilal Nehru answered Birkenhead's claim that Indians
were incapable of devising their own constitutional reforms by
formulating a scheme for Dominion status, the British ignored his
report.[39] It was at this point that the second Labour government
was formed. Once it became clear that this event had made no
difference, Gandhi announced a new campaign of non-cooperation.

British strategy was to retain real power on the subcontinent while
surrendering any number of dispensable outworks and fortifications.
A significant minority of the Conservative Party, however, opposed
concessions of any kind and charged Baldwin with betrayal. Indeed
it opposed everything from the Statute of Westminster (1931) –

which merely accepted the fact of self-government by the Dominions – to those judicious manoeuvres in India, Egypt and elsewhere to which we have already referred. Churchill was one of these fanatics, opposed to any apparent loosening of the British grip. He denounced the withdrawal of British troops from Cairo to the Canal Zone in Egypt in 1929, for example, for striking 'an immediate blow to our prestige throughout the East'. The National Government's Indian policy – constitutional change at a glacial speed and with divisive intent to further delay independence – was complete anathema to him and was portrayed in his speeches as a surrender of the British position.

Nobody would guess from such Die-hard reasoning that Stanley Baldwin had told the Conservative Party conference in 1929 that Britain's 'progress depends on our capacity to visualise the Empire, the Dominions and the Colonies alike, as one eternal and indestructible unit for production, for consumption, for distribution'.[40] Such professions of imperial virtue included an assurance to the Conservative Party Central Union on 4 December 1934 that Britain had no intention of renouncing power in India. 'It is my considered judgement', Baldwin told his audience, 'that you have a good chance of keeping the whole of that subcontinent of India in the Empire for ever.'[41] Baldwin's opinion was nothing more than what the most prominent member of the Conservative delegation, Samuel Hoare, had said at the time of the Round Table conference four years earlier. As the conference considered the Simon report, the Cabinet concurred with Hoare's plan for giving 'a semblance of responsible government and yet retain in our hands the realities and verities of British control'.[42] Lord Irwin, the Viceroy who had caused consternation in the Conservative Party by openly talking about 'Dominion status' in 1929, had explained privately to Leo Amery that this 'semblance of responsible government' was what he had in mind. What was really required, he explained, 'is some facade which will leave the essential mechanism of power still in our hands' while catering for that 'Indian psychology ... composed in equal parts of vanity, inferiority complex and fear of real responsibility'.[43]

This was what the British had hoped to achieve in Egypt when it declared that country independent in 1922. The colonial relationship still held in reality, allowing Britain to maintain a military occupation, control the country's economic affairs, and exclude it from the League of Nations and prevent differences of opinion between Britain and Egypt being treated as international disputes. In practice, for all the Die-hard complaints of weakness, Britain continued to use coercion to suppress nationalist activity in Egypt and India throughout the 1930s. Even as the Die-hards accused it of scuttle, the National Government several times resorted to martial law in India. It answered Gandhi's non-cooperation campaign with 40,000 arrests and other measures of repression in 1931–32. Some 200,000 police were employed in British India, the bulk of them under British officers.[44] London was forced to recognise, however, what the Die-hards would not see: coercion alone was not enough. When the government published a White Paper in 1933 outlining plans for constitutional reform in India, along the lines recommended by the Simon Commission, Churchill and his co-thinkers denounced this artful obstruction to independence as a British surrender. More to the point, nearly 30 per cent of the Conservative Central Council and party conference supported him in 1933 and almost half opposed the Indian reform proposals when they were put before the 1934 party conference.[45]

Clive Ponting, who notes Churchill's esteem for Mussolini's Italy at this time, is perhaps exaggerating when he argues that the Die-hard logic pointed to a fascist 'solution' in India and Egypt. Even so, Samuel Hoare, the Secretary of State for India, argued as much at the time when he told the Viceroy, Lord Willingdon, in 1933 that Churchill thought Britain was 'going Fascist' and envisaged governing India as Mussolini governed north Africa.[46] Of course Britain did not go fascist – though Churchill openly hankered after the abandonment of what he called 'complete democracy' in a series of newspaper articles published during the early 1930s[47] – and so the domestic conditions for massive repression of colonial dissidents did not exist. Such a policy would, in any case, have involved deploying bigger forces than Britain's overstretched resources would allow. The political elite in Britain had considerable faith in the policy it had adopted since the first decade of the century: the mix of concessions and coercion which we have described. It was, after all, the successful formula for managing the lower orders at home. Britain itself had gone as far as political democracy without the survival of the propertied elite and the dominance of its political representatives being called into question.

Not that democracy was what the British had in mind for India. The British order in India was maintained by a variety of singularly reactionary devices which the Simon Commission proposals were calculated to strengthen. It had been careful to enlist the support of traditional power-holders such as the Indian princes whose principalities – 563 in number – occupied an area of 712,000 square miles, covering two-fifths of India with a population of over 80 million or nearly one-quarter of the total. The British enjoyed loyal support from this feudatory quarter since many of the royal houses would have ceased to exist without British protection. Just over one hundred of the most important princes were directly brought together in the Chamber of Princes which the British invented in the 1920s, with another 127 states indirectly represented.

The federal constitution which evolved from the Simon Commission proposals and was later projected by the Government of India Act of 1935, envisaged the princes taking two-fifths of the representation in the Upper House and one-third in the Lower House. Their role as a check on the democratic threat of the Indian National Congress was thus perfectly transparent, so much so, in fact, that in the event the princes themselves were too fearful to join in the scheme when it was finally applied in 1937.

In addition to this non-elected, massively over-represented reactionary bloc, the constitution contained a number of other devices to emasculate the nationalists which were applied. In the Lower House or Federal Assembly – that is, the more popular of the two Houses of the Federal Legislature – only 86 of the 375 seats were generally open to election, and even these were only indirectly filtered through from provincial assemblies resting on an electoral base of about one-ninth of the population. The rest of the seats, apart from those that went to the princes' nominees, were allocated on a communal basis. Thus Muslims, 'scheduled castes', Sikhs, Anglo-Indians, Europeans, and Indian Christians were some of the categories catered for. On other occasions – for example in allocating the seats on the Viceroy's Executive Council – the British found artificial and minute communal divisions to add to the list. By far the most useful to them, however, was the Muslim–Hindu divide, though it was not until the Second World War that it fulfilled its manipulative potential. Until then aggregations such as the Muslim League, claiming exclusive powers of representation, were encouraged, as indeed were non-sectarian aggregations of landlords, business and commercial interests;[48] they could all be invoked to support British rule and confound the nationalists.

In British sub-Saharan Africa nothing on the scale of the problem developing in India had been encountered in the 1920s and colonial rule was considered permanent. Notwithstanding the official doctrine of 'native paramountcy', institutionalised racism operated to keep Africans in permanent subordination. It was most obvious in the settler colonies where indirect rule amounted to rule by the European minority. Indeed Southern Rhodesia, as mentioned in the last chapter, was formally governed by its white Legislative Assembly from 1923 and embarked on a South African model of discrimination as exemplified by the Land Apportionment Act of 1930, which gave the 48,000 Europeans the lion's share of the land and segregated the population on racial lines. In Kenya the European monopoly of the best farming land, coupled with strict residential segregation under the pretext of sanitation regulations inspired by South African precedent, was encouraged during Churchill's time at the Colonial Office. The Kenyan whites were only prevented from going even further towards a South African settlement by organised internal opposition – notably from the Indian community in the early 1920s – supported by humanitarian groups in Britain.

Indirect rule promised cheap administration by a tiny British elite – one British administrator per 100,000 Africans in Nigeria for example – for the protection of Britain's economic and strategic interests at the least disturbance to local communities. In Kenya, however, the settler presence required a much bigger administration, chiefly as a consequence of European demands for cheap African labour and the policing problems caused by the corresponding disruption of the rural communities from which it was drawn. Everywhere, of course, mining and plantations, the development of ports and other urban areas generated migrant labour; or at any rate they did so with the assistance of taxation policies designed to force each household to earn some money. In Kenya, for example, of the £1m earned by Kenyans in registered employment during the period 1920–23, taxes accounted for £750,000.[49] The fact that this labour was drawn from peasant households engaged in subsistence agriculture permitted its more ruthless exploitation because it was understood that the household was not entirely dependent on wages for its survival. Wallerstein argues that the maintenance of such low-cost labour forces therefore entailed the cultivation of semi-proletarian, rather than proletarian, households.[50] In this enterprise, the colonial system in Africa succeeded wonderfully well. The Sierra Leone Development Company, for example, a chief beneficiary of the 1929 Colonial Development Act, paid its workers in the iron mines between 4d and 1s per day. The United Africa Company paid as little as 4d for an 11–14-hour day.[51] Nigerian coal-miners received 1s per day for underground work, tin-miners were paid 3s 6d. It was the same in the mines of South Africa, Northern Rhodesia and the Gold Coast: inflated dividends for shareholders and repression when the workers rebelled, as in the Copper Belt explosion of 1935.[52]

The Depression led to a catastrophic collapse of commodity prices in Africa as elsewhere. In East Africa the principal cash crops fell by 70 per cent of their 1929 prices by 1932. West African raw cocoa was sold for just over 28 per cent of its 1920 price by 1939; cocoa farmers rose up in protest in 1930–31 and 1937–38. Customs receipts fell by as much as a third. Manufactured import prices, however, fell by much less with the result that the terms of trade moved against African producers. Colonial authorities responded by exhorting African peasants to produce more while balancing their own budgets in accordance with economic orthodoxy. African employees in the lower echelons of colonial adminstration were the first to lose their jobs; in the Gold Coast, for example, these low-income employees were reduced from 20,239 in 1929 to 12,572 in 1930.[53] Balanced budgets also required expenditure cuts affecting the already meagre services supplied to the African population. Colonial administrations were saddled with enormous debts incurred for state projects, but less revenue from import and export levies. Servicing these debts absorbed a growing proportion of state revenues. In Nigeria and Kenya the ratio of debt charges to gross revenue rose from 14 per cent and 18 per cent respectively in 1926 to 33 per cent and 34 per cent in 1934.[54] Tax collection was intensified and African peasants continued to pay the largest proportion of tax revenues. In Kenya in 1931, for example, Europeans paid a total of £42,596 in direct taxes, while the African population contributed £530,877.[55]

There was no prospect of Britain fulfilling its trusteeship obligations under these circumstances. Not that the 1920s had been any better from this point of view. The colonies were always expected to be self-supporting. Direct British government investment in the colonies was always minimal – the Gezira irrigation project, which made a significant impact on Sudanese cotton production by the mid-1920s, is a rare exception to this rule.[56] 'Development' of the colonies, in so far as it occurred, owed nothing to the Colonial Office, beyond the odd railway or harbour which an activist like Amery managed to squeeze out of the Treasury. Social welfare schemes, financed by colonial administrations, were similarly retarded. By 1938, for example, under 5 per cent of Nigerian children went to school. As Bernard Porter observes, 'overall government expenditure on economic development and social welfare in "black" Africa was never more than a few shillings per head of population per annum; in 1936–7 typically between 3s and 8s, with Nyasaland, Tanganyika, Nigeria, and Sierra Leone getting substantially less and only Zanzibar, Bechuanaland and Swaziland getting more. For the West Indies a Royal Commission set up in 1938 painted an almost identical picture of past neglect.'[57]

Since Britain had taken upon itself the 'dual mandate' in tropical Africa and by its own propaganda raised the expectation of colonial development, the actual stagnation of its Crown Colonies in particular represented a major embarrassment. In the United States the British Empire had few friends, while Soviet propaganda predictably dwelt on the contrast between British exploitation of the colonies and the socialist construction which was widely believed to have raised standards in the backward areas of the former Tsarist Empire. In the 1930s the weapon of criticism threatened to turn into the criticism of weapons as great power rivalries intensified. It did not help that fascist Italy wanted an empire of its own or that militarist Japan stressed its high moral purpose, its racial and cultural mission in overseas expansion, much as Britain had done before it.[58] Nazi ideology of course stressed the theory of 'Aryan' racial supremacy and the Hitler regime indulged in its own criticisms of British imperialism for denying *lebensraum* to everybody else. Such propaganda caused discomfort, as did the family resemblance of Nazi race doctrines and the practice of race discrimination in British colonies.[59] Worse still from the imperialist standpoint – though this would take time to mature – the economic depression stimulated opposition to British colonialism throughout the Empire.

Across the Caribbean, for example, a series of labour revolts shook colonialism from 1934, beginning in British Honduras and Trinidad. In every instance they revealed the same picture of grinding poverty, ruthless exploitation and mass discontent. In British Honduras the 'disturbances' began with a campaign for unemployment relief and fair wages; in Trinidad first sugar workers, then oil workers took to the streets in protest against low wages and excessive hours; the strike movement then spread to British Guiana, St Vincent, St Lucia and St Kitts; by 1937 Trinidad was the scene of even more extensive protests and the following year Jamaica experienced a sustained rebellion lasting from April to June.[60] A stronger trade unionism emerged from these struggles in Trinidad, Barbados and Jamaica. But so did evidence that was so damning of the economic and social conditions in which the mass of people lived that it was impossible to ignore even by observers predisposed to think in terms of 'agitators and trouble-makers'. Thus the Royal Commission appointed in 1938 under Lord Moyne produced a report at the end of 1939 showing wages in the countryside to be little higher than they were when the slaves were emancipated. It revealed the verminous, insanitary, overcrowded conditions of the towns; the 'chronic sickness' that was 'common' among the people; the shocking lack of health and educational facilities.[61] The Moyne Report was witheld from publication until 1945.

One of its authors was the General Secretary of the British Trades Union Congress (TUC), Walter Citrine, a man who, along with Ernest Bevin, had successfully struggled since the general strike of 1926 to rehabilitate the TUC as the authoritative voice of British labour. This was an exercise which involved marginalising, if not eliminating, 'unofficial' or spontaneous industrial militancy. The TUC took an interest in colonial labour in the wake of the Caribbean riots and by 1938 had taken the initiative in conferring 'associate' status on colonial unions which met its rigorous definition of what trade unionism was all about. In issuing model rules for colonial trade unions that specifically discouraged grass roots activity and promoted a 'responsible' and 'constitutional' approach, the TUC made the same assumptions as the Colonial Office. Indeed from the summer of 1940 steps were taken by the Colonial Office to enlist the TUC in an enterprise of sustained cooperation along these lines. The TUC was thus engaged in work which sought to depoliticise colonial unions and which eventually abetted the suppression of radical unions in Sierra Leone, Malaya and Kenya. This reflected its own acceptance of British imperialism and the illegitimacy of attempts to end it by force. Though genuinely concerned to advance the rights of colonial workers, it did so within this framework, and those who accepted its advice might not have done so had they known that it acted as an agent of the British state.[62]

The revolt in the Caribbean which stimulated TUC interest in the colonies was, of course, not unconnected to the world situation in the 1930s. The economic depression intensified the economic distress of the people, while the rise of fascism produced evidence that the age of European conquest was far from over. The Italian invasion of Abyssinia, in particular, aroused anger and fear and a sense of solidarity among peoples of African origin throughout the world. Italian aggression against Abyssinia – one of the very few African countries not under imperial rule – began in December 1934 with armed clashes on the borders of Italian Somaliland and was referred to the League of Nations by Abyssinia in January 1935. Thus by the time representatives of the French, British and Italian governments met at Stresa in April 1935 (in response to Germany's formal repudiation of the military clauses of the Versailles Treaty), Mussolini's designs on the country were clear enough to deserve at least a mention. But the Abyssinian affair was ignored and the Italians came away from the Stresa discussions with no sense of British or French opposition to their designs on the country.

Britain's role in the Italian conquest of Abyssinia was conditioned by the contradictions in its political role which the rise of rival imperialisms brought to the surface. There was an undeniable logic in acquiescing, if not actually conniving, in the Italian annexation. Mussolini, we have already noted, was admired in British political circles and his advent in 1922 had done nothing to disturb good Anglo-Italian relations. But Japanese expansionism in the Far East since the invasion of Manchuria in 1931 and the threat to the European status quo posed by the Hitler regime after 1933 brought forward the dreaded prospect of a war to defend British imperial interests in both theatres. The French government, meanwhile, was preoccupied with the Nazi state on its borders and did not want to make additional enemies. There was an obvious case for avoiding the alienation of Italy in these circumstances, especially in view of Britain's own military unpreparedness. Sir Robert Vansittart, head of the Foreign Office, was the leading advocate of this line of policy.

However, the National Government was also stuck with the fact that Abyssinia had referred the Italian aggression to the League of Nations, an organisation which now embodied popular hopes for the resolution of conflict by the collective action of its member states. Japan had already successfully called the bluff of the League in 1931, when it invaded China. British public opinion – as revealed by the

results of the widely publicised Peace Ballot in June 1935 –
nevertheless continued to believe in its potential for collective
security. In an election year the government could hardly ignore
the Peace Ballot's overwhelming verdict of popular support for
economic and non-military action against aggressors. Nor could
it rule out the possibility that allowing an Italian annexation of
Abyssinia would provoke trouble for Britain in its own colonies.
All the fancy phrases of the Covenant of the League of Nations would
be blown apart, including colonial trusteeship. The League would
stand exposed as a sham.

Britain's response, in the summer of 1935, was to try to satisfy
Mussolini with a 'compromise' that would allow Abyssinia to
survive at the price of losing a large chunk of its territory, while
simultaneously reminding Italy of British support for the League
and its opposition to outright aggression. The fascist government
was not impressed; the French under Pierre Laval had already gone
further down the road of appeasement the previous January, when
privately agreeing to an Italian take-over. By September the British
government, faced with an imminent Italian war of conquest,
publicly announced its intention to uphold the Covenant of the
League of Nations, when Hoare affirmed that it would support
collective action against an aggressor. At the same time Britain and
France also agreed to avoid any sanction that might lead to war
with Italy. Fully apprised of this last equivocation, Italy's attack
was launched on 3 October and the following month the League
applied economic sanctions. The one commodity that Mussolini
needed for his military campaign – oil – was, however, omitted from
sanctions in accordance with the policy of avoiding war in Europe.

But now that the lukewarm threat of collective action had failed,
the British and French foreign ministers produced the eponymous
Hoare–Laval proposals which involved the ceding of 60,000 square
miles (three-fifths) of Abyssinian territory to Italy. The Cabinet
approved this plan in December 1935, but almost immediately
disowned it when the details were leaked to the press, detonating
'an explosion of moral indignation in Britain of a violence and
magnitude never before seen'.[63] The extent of the outrage derived
quite simply from the fact that British policy had failed to satisfy
anyone. The Hoare–Laval intrigue served to underline both the
incapacity of the League, under its present leadership, and Britain's
inability to stand up to aggression in the conventional way.
Conservative opinion in Britain was appalled by the weakness that
was revealed in this kowtowing to Italy, while advocates of the League
saw great power connivance in the subjugation of a defenceless
people. During the next six months the Abyssinians were finally
subdued with the assistance of chemical warfare and the futile
sanctions were formally lifted in June 1936, when the process was

completed. Mussolini achieved his objective and the League was
effectively redundant.

Ever since the onset of the world crisis at the end of 1929, the
Empire had increasingly been seen both as the best bet for reversing
the alarming collapse of British trade – visible and invisible – and
as a military liability. The relative increase in inter-imperial trade
after Ottawa was a partial vindication of the first view, while the
simultaneous rise of Japan in the Far East and the fascist powers
in Europe underlined the latter. Defence spending had collapsed
in the 1920s from £766m in 1919–20 to £102m in 1932. It
represented about 10 per cent of public expenditure, as compared
to nearly 30 per cent in 1913. Social service expenditure on the
other hand had risen from 33 to 46.6 per cent in the same period,
or from just over £100m in 1913 to £497m by 1933. This reflected
the social costs of Britain's economic contractions and the coming
of political democracy. The relative ease with which Britain could
conduct its imperial affairs in the 1920s had made cuts in military
spending relatively painless and the general revulsion against war
in the last years of the decade had also made them popular. But
official caution about rearmament in the 1930s also betrayed the
weakness of the 'fourth arm of defence' – the economy. The
Treasury admitted this even when it sought to deny it. Its logic, as
Reynolds observes, was that 'the Empire's commercial and financial
strength would again be the main means of victory in another long
war and that Germany lacked this stamina. Thus it was essential
not to dissipate Britain's strength by hasty rearmament, which
would upset foreign confidence and draw heavily on imports of
machinery and raw materials – in both cases diminishing the
precious reserves'.[64]

But as Japan invaded China, Britain was in the throes of the 1931
political and economic crisis. Afflicted by growing unemployment,
the collapse of the gold standard, cuts in public expenditure and
a sterling crisis, the British were also aware of their military
incapacities in the Far East. The British navy was no longer able
to dominate the oceans, and sea-power was in any case of less
strategic value in an age of air warfare. The essence of the British
problem, however, was that a country with a shrinking relative
strength against all the key economic indicators was still hanging
on to about one-quarter of the globe. In 1932 the Ten-Year Rule
was formally abandoned and the work on the naval fortification at
Singapore – casualty of past economies – was reactivated, but only
with a consciousness that full-scale rearmament threatened national
bankruptcy. Nothing was done until Hitler pulled Germany out
of both the Disarmament Conference at Geneva and the League
of Nations in October 1933. Rearmament was initiated by the report
of the Defence Rearmament Sub-Committee in February 1934.

Its expenditure proposals were subsequently reduced at the insistence of the Chancellor, Neville Chamberlain. Fears of the scale and speed of German rearmament had to be set against fears that a too-rapid rearmament at home would enfeeble the nation by the time a war actually broke out.

In fact defence expenditure rose by about 5 per cent each year up to 1936, and over 40 per cent annually thereafter until the total in 1939 represented 18 per cent of gross national product compared to only 3 per cent in 1932–33. There was no consistent policy, however. The courtship of Mussolini produced the worst combination of outcomes, as we have seen, and continued obtusely until 1939. The Anglo-German Naval Treaty of June 1935 allowed Hitler to build a navy of up to 35 per cent the strength of Britain's in a spirit of appeasement which took no account of French fears or the likelihood of German compliance with the treaty's conditions. When, on 27 February 1936, the French Chamber of Deputies ratified the Franco-Soviet Treaty of mutual assistance, signed the previous May, the British government redoubled its efforts to appease Hitler while seeking to oppose any strengthening of the alliance between France and the Soviet Union. Hitler's military occupation of the Rhineland in March – though it had been demilitarised under the Treaty of Versailles – made no difference to these lines of British policy.

Yet a realignment of Soviet policy had been visible since the end of 1933. In September of the following year the communist state entered the League of Nations, after months of diplomatic preparations. British distaste for the Soviet Union was scarcely concealed, however, and was well expressed by Baldwin when he privately commented in July 1936 that 'If there is any fighting to be done I should like to see the Bolsheviks and Nazis doing it ... if he [Hitler] moves East, I shall not break my heart'.[65] Baldwin's wishful thinking came a step closer to reality when the Anti-Comintern Pact was concluded the following November, though the danger presented by Germany and Japan had long since been evident to both the Russians and the British. Vansittart had accurately summarised Soviet fears in a memorandum of 21 February 1935 in which he said that Stalin's government had only two enemies of real significance – Germany and Japan. These were the same two enemies that Britain faced. And yet the entry of the Soviet Union into the League of Nations had occasioned no new thinking in Britain of how Russian military forces figured in the balance of power. British intelligence continued to focus on the communist threat until the mid-1930s[66] and the Chiefs of Staff continued to ponder the Russian danger to India as before.[67] Well before Stalin decapitated the Red Army in 1937–39, Soviet forces were otherwise considered irrelevant.

Up to the spring of 1939 British diplomacy made no effort to reach mutual defence agreements with the Soviet Union. Any such arrangement would actually stand in the way of the appeasement of Germany and bring forward British involvement in a European war. When civil war broke out in Spain in July 1936, following General Franco's attempt to overthrow the Republic, the avoidance of a general European war was the official reason given for Britain's policy of non-intervention. Britain successfully pressurised Leon Blum's Popular Front government in France to take the same line, even though Germany and Italy intervened in support of Franco. It was probably at this juncture that Mussolini's foreign policy finally inclined towards Hitler; but if the Spanish Civil War united the fascist states, it served to expose divisions in Britain. The governing party – the Conservatives – clearly had no love for the Republic and detested socialism. Some of them had openly admired Mussolini and harboured sympathies for Nazi Germany. The British Left doubted their urgency in resisting Hitler; so did Hitler.

It was, however, impossible by 1936 for the Cabinet to entertain any illusions about the nature of the Nazi regime. Britain's global interests had not confused the issue in 1914, nor could they now. The country could not long hold on to its Empire if Germany dominated Europe. That much was clear. But the Empire did not help in deciding what to do about it. The Chiefs of Staff annual review for 1937 noted the military danger at 'both ends' of the Empire and the loss of security in its (Mediterranean) middle. They saw that 'only very great military and financial strength' could give the Empire security – but this was what Britain lacked.[68] It was impossible to act alone, then, but highly dangerous to make allies like those nurtured by France in Eastern Europe. A formal commitment in Eastern Europe might suck Britain into a European war at somebody else's convenience and bring forward the moment when Japan could attack in the exposed Far Eastern extreme.

The Colonial Secretary, Ormsby Gore, was informed as early as December 1937, furthermore, that any war between Japan and the British Empire would elicit considerable sympathy for Japan in Burma, and what was true here could apply elsewhere in the region.[69] This was at a time when the military planners were actually anticipating a Japanese offensive in South Asia and even had the foresight to see that it could come on land down the Malayan peninsula.[70] The Chiefs of Staff had to consider all possibilities, of course, at a moment in the decay of British power when even a war with Italy represented a considerable strategic problem. Considerations of imperial defence were always to the fore, such as the defence of the Middle East and the route to India, and conflict with Italy could only divert resources that were needed to protect Britain from Nazi Germany.

The existence of a sprawling Empire, then, did not 'distract' British attention from Europe, so much as reinforce the conviction that any war could be disastrous for Britain. It was a conviction based on the fact that the last great conflagration had bankrupted the economy and left permanent scars in the national psyche. And it was supported by the Dominions, which had their own strategic considerations to make and their own memories of 1914–18.[71] Munich was like Chanak all over again in so far as it made clear the determination of the Dominions not to be bound to fight because of a British inability to keep the peace.

## CHAPTER 4

# War, National Bankruptcy and Imperial Development, 1939–45

When war against Hitler's Germany finally came British politicians were almost immediately faced with the problem which had taken three years of total war to develop after 4 August 1914: national bankruptcy. Although the nightmare of a war on two fronts had yet to materialise, the Cabinet was warned as early as 8 September 1939 that Britain's total resources were 'vastly inferior' to 1914 and that exhaustion of Britain's gold reserves would soon 'render us incapable of waging war if war is prolonged'.[1] Yet the country was simply incapable of self-sufficiency in armaments and raw materials and the United States had legislated against the 1917 option of war loans, requiring instead that Britain paid cash for everything. In 1939 the United States had already sold Britain 8,364 machine tools, as crucial as any commodity in the age of industrialised warfare; in the following two years it supplied about one-third of the total British requirement. It was the passage through Congress of the Lend-Lease Act in March 1941 which made this (and the supply of many other essential goods) possible and allowed Britain to survive – but only in a condition of extreme material dependency on the United States.[2]

With the imminent collapse of France in May 1940, the newly installed coalition government headed by Churchill considered the alternative of a negotiated peace. As the Foreign Secretary, Lord Halifax, pointed out, there was no question now of defeating Germany, but it might still be possible to preserve the Empire. The trouble was, as became clear the more the Cabinet considered the matter, there was no reason to believe that Hitler would settle for domination of Central Europe. Indeed, there was no reason to believe in the permanence of any compromise with Hitler at all. It was better to struggle on in the hope that he would overstretch himself and that the Americans would enter the war. Britain's own strategic over-extension meant, of course, that it was already living on hope of protection from the American fleet in the Far East – a weakness (given the absence of any actual American commitment) which the Japanese exploited in August 1940 by successfully pressing for the withdrawal of all British troops from their garrisons in southern

China. Such was Britain's extremity that summer, as it faced Germany alone, that Churchill – obdurate Unionist that he was – agreed to make a declaration in favour of a united Ireland if Ireland abandoned its neutrality.

These negotiations failed for precisely the same reason that Britain was unable to persuade Indian nationalists to support the war effort: the deal involved 'jam tomorrow' in return for immediate sacrifices and neither de Valera nor Gandhi could trust the British to honour their pledges. It was only a matter of months, in fact, since Churchill had argued for the use of force to reclaim the Treaty Ports reserved for British use since the Partition but handed back to the Irish against his bitter opposition in 1938. For their part the Indian National Congress and the elected members of the central legislature had been brutally reminded of their lowly place in the great imperial 'chain of being' on 3 September 1939 when the government of India declared the subcontinent at war with Germany without so much as going through the motions of consultation. Despite the strong anti-fascist sympathies of Gandhi and Nehru, this arrogant act might have been calculated to alienate Congress. Lord Linlithgow, the Viceroy, refused furthermore to specify British war aims in relation to India, privately explaining his reluctance to Lord Zetland, the Secretary of State, in terms of his conviction that the day of Indian independence was 'very remote' and 'the least we say about it in all probability the better'.[3] The Chamberlain Cabinet had declared itself in agreement with this policy by deciding in October 1939 both that there would be no constitutional change during the war and that Congress would be denied the right to construct its own system of government at the end of it.

Needless to say, Churchill, who took over the Premiership in May 1940, fully concurred in this attitude but was obliged to modify the British government's position as the war took its disastrous course. With the benefit of hindsight we can say that by the end of 1941 Britain's survival was virtually guaranteed because of the German invasion of the Soviet Union on 22 June and the Japanese attack against the American Pacific fleet at Pearl Harbor on 7 December. Henceforth the Red Army occupied above 90 per cent of Nazi forces and Britain could confidently rely on the overwhelming might of the United States, once it was fully mobilised. But the British experience between the fall of France in June 1940 and the end of 1941 had been uniformly grim. It has already been established that by August 1940 the country was bankrupt and at the mercy of American goodwill. That very month the United States demanded military bases on Bermuda, Newfoundland and on five of Britain's Caribbean colonies in exchange for ships. From the first mention of Lend-Lease the following December, it was made clear that there would be no help under that programme until Britain had sold all of its assets in the United States. The Americans refused, furthermore, to defend British interests in the Far East. With its economy just able to function thanks to Lend-Lease and a record of almost continuous military reversals stretching throughout its first 18 months, the coalition government was faced with an imminent assault on its Far Eastern possessions in the last month of 1941, Japan having already taken possession of southern Indo-China the previous July. And still the government had failed to come to terms with the leaders of Indian nationalism.

Yet in August 1941 Churchill – in the Atlantic Charter – was obliged to support an American statement of war aims which affirmed the right of colonial peoples to national sovereignty and self-determination. Churchill specifically denied the application of these principles of the Atlantic Charter to the British Empire, though Attlee – and more to the point, Roosevelt – affirmed their relevance. When Hong Kong fell to the Japanese in December 1941, and the fall of Malaya and the 'fortress' of Singapore came hard on its heels, only to be followed by the loss of Burma, the indifference if not the antipathy of the local peoples towards the blessings of British imperialism was widely commented upon. The *Times*'s Singapore correspondent concluded, in a famous dispatch (18 February 1942), that despite its 120-year dominance, 'British rule and culture and the small British community formed no more than a thin and brittle veneer' in Malaya where 'the vast majority of Asiatics were not sufficiently interested in the continuance of this rule to take any steps to ensure its continuance'. An altogether different lesson worried the British government, however. Churchill was not alone in his shock that these colonies could be lost to an inferior race and that European prestige could be dealt such a blow in the region; among officials and politicians alike, both in Britain and the United States, 'a pervasive racial arrogance' held sway 'which relegated not only the Japanese but all Asians to the second class and lower'.[4] Racism naturally blinded its proponents to the reality of nationalism in Asia just as surely as it helped to produce it in the first place. But by February 1942, with the possible loss of Ceylon and large chunks of India on the horizon, something had to be done to appease the nationalists.

The Indian National Congress's refusal to cooperate with the British had led to the resignation of the provincial ministries in October 1939 and to measures of repression (with 14,000 nationalists imprisoned by May 1941). The policy of divide and rule was also put on to a higher plane. The British recognised the Muslim League – which for its own reasons was prepared to support the war effort – as the sole authoritative voice of India's Islamic population, diverse and dispersed throughout the subcontinent as that was. Mohammed Ali Jinnah was encouraged to regard himself as the possessor of a veto on any political settlement which failed to satisfy the League, with its recently formulated and wholly nebulous demand for Pakistan. This official opportunism undoubtedly helped to transform the League – which had won only 109 of the 482 communal seats allotted to Muslims in the elections of 1937 – into a real political force by 1945, though it would be foolish to think that that was all there was to it. Nevertheless the British, who did not want a partitioned subcontinent in 1947, certainly assisted the process which brought it about.

After the loss of Singapore, the calamitous strategic position Britain was now faced with forced Churchill to at least give the appearance of seeking that political settlement which Roosevelt, Chiang Kai-Shek, and the Left in Britain had pressed for as the best way to achieve the full mobilisation of India. Even Leo Amery, the new Secretary of State and firm imperialist, had seen the need for a statement of India's post-war Dominion status as long ago as July 1940 but had been blocked by the Prime Minister. Now, in March 1942, Churchill was forced to allow Stafford Cripps to go to India armed with a Draft Declaration promising Dominion status. Of course the Indian National Congress wanted full independence and objected to the provisions in Cripps's proposals which gave the princely states the right to forward nominees instead of elected representatives to a future constituent assembly and the right to reach separate agreements with Britain regarding their future status. The Indians also wanted a real say in the defence of the country and Cripps advised the Cabinet to give the appearance of concession on this remaining stumbling block as negotiations proceeded. But neither Churchill nor the Viceroy Lord Linlithgow were prepared to contemplate having to share power with an Indian Cabinet and Cripps was forced to return to Britain in April having been substantially undermined by the Prime Minister. Churchill meanwhile refused to put Roosevelt's message asking for renewed negotiations before the Cabinet, threatening the President with damaged Anglo-American relations and his own retirement from politics if he persisted.[5]

The failure of the Cripps Mission paved the way for the Quit India campaign of civil disobedience which Gandhi led from August 1942. Critics of British policy in India likened it to 'one of the worst military fiascoes of the war', such was the scale of its ineptitude and lack of imagination.[6] As a matter of fact the Allied military position in the region improved after the summer of 1942, though no thanks to the War Cabinet's India policy. For the political situation in India deteriorated markedly. Linlithgow made known his intention to respond to any campaign by the Indian National Congress with 'a declared determination to crush the organisation as a whole'.[7] By the end of 1942 serious disorder throughout the subcontinent had been answered by over 60,000 arrests and virtual martial law. Nine hundred had died in August alone and as many as 42,000 defected to the Indian National Army to fight alongside the Japanese. Nehru, arrested on 9 August, was jailed until 15 June 1945. As Churchill said at the Lord Mayor's banquet on 10 November 1942, he had 'not become the King's Minister in order to preside over the liquidation of the British Empire'. Yet for all Churchill's bluster, the mass repression of August 1942 brought the end of the Raj a step closer; it was impossible now for the Indian National Congress to contemplate an agenda containing anything less than complete independence.

This was not how it was seen from London. The almost customary incomprehension of Asian nationalism of the politicians and officials responsible for policy carried well into the post-war era. It could hardly be otherwise given the dominance in government of men who knew little about the peoples and places they governed except that they were 'lesser breeds without the law'. For example, the Secretary of State for India, Leo Amery, told Linlithgow just before he was replaced as Viceroy by General Wavell in October 1943:

> If India is to be really capable of holding its own in the future without direct British control from outside, I am not sure that it will not need an increasing fusion of stronger Nordic blood, whether by settlement or intermarriage or otherwise. Possibly it has been a real mistake of ours in the past not to encourage Indian Princes to marry English wives for a succession of generations and so breed a more virile type of native ruler.[8]

The fact that this nonsense was uttered in the middle of a war against a racist state is surprising enough. But Amery was actually rather clear-sighted over India by comparison with the Prime Minister. Indeed they clashed over India when Amery proposed acceptance of Dominion status in July 1940. On that occasion Amery also complained that he received no support from Attlee in Cabinet.[9] Attlee was certainly capable of questioning imperial policies himself of course, though – as Amery's story suggests – without any consistency. He argued in Cabinet on one occasion, for example, that the colonies only benefited a small 'capitalist group' whilst imposing defence burdens and wars upon the entire British electorate. In September 1942 he proposed the international control and administration of the colonies, much as the Americans desired.[10] In March, as chair of the Cabinet Committee on India, he even devised a scheme for constitutional reform in India designed to find a way out of the mess created in September 1939. The Cabinet's resulting deadlock over these proposals was resolved by, and helped to prompt, the Cripps Mission.

Yet the failure of the Cripps Mission also led Attlee to deduce pessimistic conclusions about the capacity of India for self-rule and he fully supported the policy of repression after August 1942. In December of the same year he found himself on the same side as the landed luminaries and successive Colonial Secretaries Viscount Cranborne and Oliver Stanley, together with the Foreign Secretary, Sir Anthony Eden, in calling on the War Cabinet to correct the 'misguided' American view that, in the words of the protestors, 'there is something archaic in the conception of the British Colonial Empire'. This has the look of a concerted propaganda offensive; for meanwhile Arthur Creech Jones, Attlee's future Colonial Secretary, faced with American criticism at an inter-governmental conference convened during the same month at Mont Tremblant in Canada – where Lord Hailey acted as chief apologist for British imperialism – rallied to the defence of British colonial policy in much the same terms. So too did his fellow-enthusiast for 'colonial development', Rita Hinden, Secretary of the Fabian Colonial Bureau.[11] Both could claim more interest in a progressive colonial policy than even Attlee and like him found no difficulty in reconciling such sympathies with continued British rule.

These attitudes are best explained as manifestations of Labour's traditional dual aproach to imperial matters – simultaneously embracing notions of trusteeship while criticising much of the actual running of the Empire. American opinion was more severe – one poll of June 1942 showed that 56 per cent of Americans agreed that the British could be described as 'oppressors' because of their exploitation of colonial possessions.[12] Roosevelt himself was a stern critic who deplored British imperialism and thus found Stalin (both at Teheran and Yalta) a more congenial ally than Churchill when discussing the future of the European colonies and their timetables for independence – a question to which he frequently returned. But the British had no intention of submitting either to timetables or to the schemes for an internationally policed trusteeship system which Roosevelt pressed for. In fact after the Yalta 'summit' (4–11 February 1945), the Armistice and Post-War Committee – which Attlee chaired – 'chose to close ranks against the Americans' precisely over this issue.[13] Little wonder then that Roosevelt expected 'more trouble with Britain after the war than we are having with Germany now'.[14]

Clearly, given Britain's dependence on the United States, the government had a major public relations problem during the war in relation to the Empire. This is one reason why the old idea of colonial 'development' came strongly into vogue; what better way to answer Roosevelt's repeated criticism of the economic stagnation of the colonies which he routinely attributed to the neglect of the imperial Powers? Indeed there was already precedent for this. After the war Creech Jones revealed something of the origins of this policy when he reminded a conference of African governors that the Colonial Development and Welfare Act of 1940 (as well as the one that followed in 1945) had been a response to the 'appalling conditions in the West Indies and the continued agitation against them', both inside and outside Parliament.[15] We saw in the last chapter that labour unrest in Trinidad and Jamaica during 1937 and 1938 brought the facts to light and even the West Indies Royal Commission was unable, despite talk of 'malcontents' and 'lawless elements', to disguise the underlying causes of poverty, low wages, unemployment and bad housing. Only £3m of the £20m made available by the Act of 1940 was spent during the next four years; impecunious Britain had hardly chosen a propitious moment to make a start, though the point rather underlines the Act's public relations function. It was obviously the thought that counted and, as parliamentary debate made clear, 'the thought' was composed of appeals to colonial solidarity in the war effort and the confounding of imperial critics, as well no doubt as the genuine hopes of the believers in trusteeship. It was also a sign, as it turned out, of the direction of colonial policy.

Development of the colonies seemed to answer almost every need. We have already seen that the lure of a more integrated Empire – one that could be put to more economic advantage than the ramshackle reality – had periodically tempted British politicians in the past, especially during times of crisis in Britain. Necessity was the mother of these dreams of exploitation. The Second World War obviously created just such an immediate emergency. But these dire circumstances also suggested that colonial development might answer the problems of post-war reconstruction in a world dominated by the United States. For reformers such as Creech Jones, however, there was also the prize of harmonious progress because schemes of colonial development represented to such minds a practical way of fulfilling Britain's obligations of trusteeship. Others were tempted by the prospect of deflecting the forces of nationalism. Three months after the launch of the Quit India campaign Cripps, for example, advised the Cabinet that:

> If the British Government could enlist the sympathy of the workers and peasants by immediate action on their behalf, the struggle in India would no longer be between Indian and British on a nationalist basis, but between the classes in India on an economic basis. There would thus be a good opportunity to rally the mass of Indian opinion to our side.[16]

It was a naive idea, of course, conceived under duress, but it was made even more unrealistic by the assumption that once bankrupt Britain had summoned up the massive resources needed to realise this project, 'the Indian workers and peasants [would] realise it is a British initiative which is working for them against their Indian oppressors'. In other words Cripps – by reputation an informed friend of India – imagined that British policy would be seen to be more representative of the mass of Indians than the leaders of the Indian National Congress.

No doubt it was the consoling thought that the nationalists were unrepresentative men-on-the-make which seduced the whole Cabinet and persuaded it to look closely at the development 'option' after August 1942. Even Amery – not one to throw money at an Indian problem – talked about the need 'for a much bolder social policy' in India. Desperate evils call for desperate remedies but this one was impossible for a bankrupt metropolis like Britain. Febrile crisis management ensured, however, that the Indian development option survived the war and, as the next chapter will show, surfaced as an alternative to independence in the minds of some leading ministers in the Attlee government. It only needs to be added that the other alternative considered by the Cabinet in 1942 – to impose on India a heavy bill for services rendered during the war and then clear out altogether – was given short shrift.[17]

The longer-term merits of colonial development exerted a stronger pull than is suggested by these *ad hoc* considerations on the deflection of Indian nationalism. British industry's interest, as represented by the Federation of British Industries, is on record from April 1942 and seems to have rested on the realisation that unless more use was made of the areas where Britain enjoyed preferential trade and political control, US domination of the world economy would become permanent. Potentially the colonies could not only supply Britain's needs for raw materials and foodstuffs, but also an effective demand for British goods. Both supply and demand depended on a strategy of development. In February 1944 the FBI believed that the importance of Empire trade was such that 'a common Empire policy' had to be formulated that 'could be advanced by the Empire as a whole in international discussions'.[18] Difficult though this might be, it was preferable either to the dominance of the dollar or revolutionising industrial efficiency at home, when every indication suggested a stronger, more militant workforce animated by costly expectations of social reform and full employment in peacetime.

These commercial considerations were informed by mounting evidence of the United States' intention to impose its own priorities on the post-war international economic order. As early as the Newfoundland conference in August 1941, the British not only had to contend with Roosevelt's interpretation of the Atlantic Charter, but also with American pressure to abandon imperial preference in return for Lend-Lease. The problem was that this American talk about self-government and free trade added up to the liquidation of the British Empire and the sterling area. Churchill put his own gloss on the Atlantic Charter (with the Cabinet's endorsement), as we have seen, and refused to concede anything more than a commitment to future discussions with the Americans on the question of a liberal world economy. But from the moment of Britain's dependency on Lend-Lease the Americans were in a position to exert some control over the British economy. This they did by insisting that Britain accept severe limitations on its ability to export – no lend-lease goods or close substitutes in competition with American goods, for example – and by ensuring that the country's gold and dollar reserves were kept within narrow limits (£150m–£250m). By these devices the United States was able to accelerate its encroachment on British markets – for example in South America – and prevent Britain from becoming strong enough to ignore American pressure for an open world economy.[19]

At the Tehran meeting of the 'Big Three' (28 November–1 December 1943) Roosevelt tried to draw Stalin into opposition to Churchill on the future of the Empire. Stalin was cagey about this invitation and turned out to be much more interested in the deal which Churchill offered at a meeting in the Kremlin in October 1944 – British support for the Soviet Union in Eastern Europe in return for Russian assistance against the Americans in the restoration of Britain's Far Eastern possessions. It was here that Churchill presented Stalin with the notorious spheres of influence scheme for the division of Eastern and Southern Europe. Roosevelt returned to the colonial problem, however, when the three met at Yalta (February 1945), where he proposed the return of Hong Kong to China, independence for Indochina and trusteeship for Korea (with the British excluded from its administration). Meanwhile, American efforts to frame the charter of the United Nations took care to include much stronger powers of inspection of trusteeship territories than the mandatory system of the League of Nations ever provided, together with acceptance of their eventual self-determination. In the event the UN did not go so far as a commitment to independence. American concerns for 'security' – which had pitched the military against Roosevelt's more idealistic plans for the post-war – finally gained the upper hand. But even the watered-down agreements still exceeded British ambitions. The UN Trusteeship Council was pledged to inspect regularly the trusteeship territories, report to the General Council, and receive petitions from the subject peoples concerned; the UN Charter also required the imperial Powers 'to develop self-government'.

British policy throughout the war was to make sure that no imperial possessions were placed under any such trusteeship scheme. But it was evident that the American case for trusteeship was fashioned to make the imperial power responsible for the economic, social and political development of its overseas possessions. It was the neglect of this responsibility, as we have seen, which so angered Roosevelt. An obvious riposte was to show that policies of colonial development were already in place; trusteeship would then be rendered superfluous and colonial independence self-defeating, since the independent former colony would deprive itself of the largesse of the imperial power. It was also clear that British influence within the informal empire of the Middle East – which had relied upon increasingly fragile mandatory rights in Palestine and Transjordan as well as bitterly contested treaties with Egypt and Iraq – would need a different foundation in a world which favoured the principle of national independence. Voices within the British foreign service reasoned that a commitment to economic development might provide that foundation. Lord Hailey, for example – the Lugard of his day – reasoned in a very influential report of 1942 that even in Africa nationalism could be anticipated as a future problem unless the educated minority was co-opted by the British into development projects.[20] If Britain emerged as the champion of the local inhabitants – or so the new logic suggested – its strategic and economic positions might be maintained, in much the same way as Cripps had envisaged in relation to India in 1942. One of the strengths of such schemes, I have already suggested, is that they were ideologically versatile, satisfying Fabian reformers as well as die-hard imperialists. Britain's own economic reconstruction, in a world dominated by America, might depend on the Empire, as the FBI saw in 1942, and the colonial development that this entailed could, without too much ingenuity, be made to answer American criticisms of imperialism. In short, the development policy had the look of a panacea.

Japan's gains in the Far Eastern empire, especially Malaya, showed the urgent need of new thinking. Few doubted Egypt's vulnerability to a Malayan show of disloyalty, if the German armies entered it. In Iraq the 32,000-man army actually rebelled against the British garrisons in May 1941. In Palestine the conflict between Arab and Jew dominated the scene, rather than any interest in supporting the British war-effort. Persian oil had to be safeguarded by a timely invasion of that country by Soviet and British forces. Indian defence required the imprisonment of Gandhi and Nehru. War needs provoked strikes on the Northern Rhodesian copperbelt and led to the proscription of the Kikuyu Central Association in Kenya on grounds of its doubtful loyalty.[21] No wonder that the Empire had figured in pre-war talk as a strategic liability. But then it also contributed five million troops – half of them Indians who were mostly deployed against the Japanese.

Africa alone contributed one million troops and carriers, including 100,000 Nigerians, 90,000 Kenyans and 86,000 Tanganyikans. Many of the soldiers concerned saw action in Burma, North Africa, East Africa and the Middle East. In 1944, by which time the British armies in Burma massively outnumbered the Japanese, 12 per cent of the troops were African, the same proportion as the British contingent; 60 per cent were Indian or Gurkha. After the war they returned home with new perspectives on the old order – the Accra riots of 1948, for example, were started by ex-sevicemen demonstrating against poor living conditions. The unsettling effects of the war were predicted well before such events erupted, but there was little that the British could do other than to go on encouraging the destabilisation. Promises were made as in the First World War. Ceylon and Malta were offered self-government, new constitutions were produced for Trinidad and British Guiana, and an African was added to the Legislative Council in Kenya. The Gold Coast was given an African majority on its Legislative Council and Trinidad was allowed the adult franchise for elections to its House of Representatives. But would such concessions suffice?

The war effort itself made this unlikely. 'Almost everywhere the intense pressure for the colonies to produce more goods to meet war needs led to more and more imperial direction over colonial economies.'[22] Laissez-faire was abandoned and state-directed production drives embarked upon which could only undermine the 'traditional' political order that indirect rule had depended upon. Further manpower was enlisted for the war effort via increased production of crops such as palm-oil, sisal and rubber, as well as work in the mines for copper or coal. 'This demand for Africa's raw materials was secured not by higher prices, but in many cases by various forms of coercion, including conscription on to plantations or into mines.'[23] In Nigeria, for example, 18,000 labourers were forced to work in the mines. But inflation was an effective indirect form of coercion in most cases because the prices received by growers were controlled by colonial governments and kept below the world market price for the commodity. 'The result was that metropolitan companies and their local agents acquired cash crops cheaply and sold imported goods at high prices, while the farmer had to produce more if he were to be able to purchase them.'[24] Meanwhile colonial governments pocketed the difference between the price paid to the producer and the world market price 'and used it to develop reserves that helped to finance the war effort'.[25]

There is no doubt that the political elites in Africa were aware of American and Soviet criticisms of colonialism. In 1941, for example, the *West African Pilot* of Lagos welcomed the Atlantic

Charter and attacked Churchill's exemption of the British Empire from its stipulations. Some new political associations were created such as Nnamdi Azikiwe's National Council of Nigeria and the Cameroons (NCNC). They tended to be dominated by commercial interests and by the rich and educated. But the changes instigated by colonial administrators touched more than just the lives of the elite. The labouring poor were hit hard by the production drives, the shortages of imports, the controls on primary producers exerted by metroplitan companies and the official marketing-board system, the increases of taxes (including the introduction of an income tax) and import duties. In Nigeria, Kenya, Northern Rhodesia and the Gold Coast the public revenue more than doubled. The net effect of these changes was to squeeze the living standards of African labourers and farmers. Organisations like the NCNC acquired a mass following, trade unions multiplied, as did strikes and 'disturbances'. In 1945 alone, major strikes broke out in Mombassa, Dar-es-Salaam, Zanzibar, Northern and Southern Rhodesia, and Nigeria (where a 44-day general strike was provoked by the high cost of living). The organised nationalist movements which had been conspicuous by their absence before 1939 came to life under these war-generated circumstances because the literate elite was able for the first time to merge its own interests with those economic and social discontents felt by the rural and urban poor. This is the main reason why the flurry of constitutional reforms embarked upon in the 1940s never went far enough, even though they exceeded the expectations of 1939.

In the Middle East nationalist agitation was long established and long repressed. As in almost every other corner of the British Empire, indirect rule had always depended on local collaborators for whom democracy and social reform were extremely distasteful. The war, however, led to a more obtrusive British presence throughout the region which succeeded in widening the gulf between the population and the cliques of British-sponsored rulers. In Iraq, for example, where a client regime was re-established after military intervention overthrew the pro-German government of Rashid Ali in spring 1941, Britain's wartime policy greatly exacerbated the situation because

> it meant the re-establishment of an undemocratic regime dominated by a small group of wealthy and repressive politicians who were unrepresentative of the country's ethnic or sectarian balance and who generally demonstrated considerably more concern for personal financial aggrandizement than for the welfare of the great bulk of the population'. This regime then permitted or accepted the stationing of large numbers of British, Indian, and Polish troops in Iraq; the transformation of Iraq's

military from a nationalist force to little more than an appendage of Britain's army; the placing of British officials in numerous important positions throughout Iraq's government; and ... a terrible inflation that enriched a small group of landowners and businessmen while impoverishing most of the rest of the population.[26]

The incoherence of Britain's development strategy in the region is self-evident once it is remembered that corrupt and detested elites of this sort were the only friends the Foreign Office enjoyed in the Middle East.

India's involuntary mobilisation for war led to a much bigger direct challenge of British rule than that of the Iraqi army. Though it was quickly suppressed in the summer of 1942, once again the necessary abandonment of *laissez-faire* and indirect rule brought British officialdom into unhappy contact with the mass of people; the prevailing shortages and inflation could only aggravate an already difficult situation. The government of India took control of grain marketing, for example, and imposed food rationing and price controls in a situation where the lack of consumer goods had encouraged hoarding. The war effort dictated the character of industrial expansion and thus actually diminished the goods available to the civilian population, leading to 'a savage increase in the price' of what was available.[27] Famine affected many parts of India but especially Bengal in 1943 and 1944, where three million people died. This was not the result of natural causes but a compound of factors derived from the war, including inflation, hoarding, the Japanese successes of 1942 (which cut off India from all the rice-producing areas of Southeast Asia), the export of food from India to the Middle East, military commandeering of transport, administrative incompetence and culpable neglect. Military censorship, furthermore, was used to remove the word 'famine' from reports of the disaster.[28]

The Viceroy warned London of approaching problems in December 1942. On 31 July 1943 Amery alerted the War Cabinet that 'the Indian economy is being strained almost to breaking point by the enormous demands laid on it in its dual role as a source of supplies and of men for the Army, and a base for military operations'. Characteristically, however, his memorandum was as much concerned to dramatise 'subversive activities' in explaining both the hoarding of grain and the effects of news of the famine on troop morale. By September Amery was concerned that the conditions in Bengal 'are becoming a serious menace to supply operations and to the movement of troops. The sight of famine conditions cannot but cause distress to the European troops and anxiety to the Indian troops as to the condition of their families in other parts of India' where conditions 'afford ample cause for anxiety'.[29] The War Cabinet was not sufficiently moved. Perhaps Amery's language had failed to move them. But Linlithgow, the Viceroy, did not even bother to visit Bengal, and Churchill, who took his advice on India from the equally racist Lord Cherwell, decided not to send relief. Amery dubbed Churchill's attitude 'Hitler-like' and Linlithgow's successor General Wavell concluded that the Prime Minister 'seemed to regard sending food to India as an "appeasement" of Congress'.[30] Indeed, Wavell's request for food was answered, according to his diary entry for 5 July 1944, by a 'peevish telegram' from Churchill 'to ask why Gandhi hadn't died yet'.[31]

By the time these remarks were recorded India had been transformed from a sterling debtor in 1939, with external sterling obligations of £350m, into Britain's single largest sterling creditor with assets of £1,300m by 1945. This had been achieved through the operation of the sterling area, the origins of which were discussed in the last chapter. The outbreak of war transformed the sterling area into a financial union managed from London. The convertibility of sterling was of course suspended for the duration and exporters to Britain were paid in credits, usually Treasury Bills. Members' reserves of gold and hard currencies were pooled and entrusted to the British Exchange Equalisation Fund which issued only such sums as it saw fit. The effect of this system was to prevent its members spending money. While the cost of 'purely Indian defence measures' was borne locally in any case – amounting to some £1,255m all told – Britain paid for the purchase of Indian stores and war materials used for the general prosecution of the war by means of credits to the account of the Reserve Bank of India held in London. The value of India's export surpluses was also retained in Britain, much of it representing substantial sales of food and raw materials to the Ministries of Food and Supply. The upshot was that the whole immediate cost of Indian defence and British purchases from India fell on the Indian people and Britain was left owing £1,300m when the war ended, which represented, as was pointed out at the time, a claim on Britain's physical and human resources equivalent to one-seventh of one year's net national income.[32]

But this was not the end of it. Britain's total debt to the sterling area stood at £3,000m by 1945, £2,500m of which was owed to Commonwealth countries, with Egypt (£400m) and Iraq (£70m) making up most of the rest. The contribution of the colonial dependencies proper (excluding India) to this system of forced borrowing stood at £454m and was rising, as we shall see, throughout the period of the Labour governments. When these sums of money are set beside the unquantified value of colonial labour pressed into the war effort, the five million colonial troops, the additional thousands of carriers, the rigged prices for colonial produce, the tax hikes and unequal exchange, and the reduced standards of living, it is plain that the involuntary contribution and sacrifice of Britain's dependencies to its war effort was considerable. It must have impressed itself particularly on those whose appetites were whetted by the thought of future colonial 'development' when the war was over.

But, as we have already remarked, privileged access to colonial resources stood in the way of the American goal of an open world economy. In February 1942 the Lend-Lease agreement had insisted on 'the elimination of all forms of discriminatory treatment in international commerce'. The State Department in particular remained convinced that American prosperity could not be sustained unless the world was opened up to US exports. This was understood to involve the destruction of the sterling bloc, which discriminated against US goods. The sterling area was the world's biggest trade zone but it operated behind imperial preference and centrally controlled allocations of dollar expenditures which could only restrict demand for US goods. Prising this system apart clearly involved abolition of imperial preference and a commitment by Britain to restore the convertibility of sterling. And so the issue was pressed again at the United Nations Monetary and Financial Conference at Bretton Woods in July 1944, where the Allies agreed on the creation of the World Bank and the International Monetary Fund. The IMF was to be dedicated to the 'harmonization of national policies' to promote a 'multilateral system of payments' and 'the elimination of foreign exchange restrictions which hamper the growth of world trade', though in the event – and much to the annoyance of the State Department – Britain successfully insisted on the preservation of exchange restrictions for another five years. But the pressure continued and, as Kolko observes, 'Everywhere, from the Middle East and Latin America to direct conferences, any discussion of foreign economic policy with the British moved from bad to worse'.[33]

To an avowed imperialist like Leo Amery, it was a clear case of the British Empire being targeted by 'US economic imperialism masquerading as a liberal trade programme'. It was the counterpart to American demands for colonial independence which the head of the Colonial Office's General Department described as 'a political catchword which has no meaning apart from economics'. 'The Americans', he argued, 'are quite ready to make their dependencies politically "independent" while economically bound hand and foot to them and see no inconsistency in this.'[34] The Western allies knew one another well. Both countries had a history of preaching free trade and the 'Open Door' and in both countries sober calculation of comparative advantage generated support for these principles.

But just as the Americans saw the British Empire as a practical departure from free trade, the British remembered American tariffs, their systematic exclusion from Western Hemisphere oil, American price-fixing policies, hypocritically combined with attacks on their own restrictive practices in the Middle East and South Asia. Furthermore, as the Federation of British Industries saw, in the circumstances generated by the war free trade meant American hegemony and British interests might be better served by maintaining the protection of the sterling bloc. The Americans had taken the opportunity provided by the war, for example, to take over traditional British markets in South America and the threat of their permanent exclusion prompted several Foreign Office complaints to the State Department in July 1943. British dependency on America, however, ruled out an open breach with its post-war masterplan. For their part, American policy-makers in the State Department realised that a crippled Britain would be no use at all in creating the multilateral trade programme which the US needed. Some of them also saw the need for a partnership against the Soviet Union, though this might mean, in the words of one business leader, 'absorption into [the] American empire of the parts of the British Empire which we will be willing to accept'.[35]

The 'parts' of particular interest from 1943 were the Middle Eastern oilfields. By the beginning of that year the US government was determined to dominate Saudi Arabia and Iran, the latter having been subject to US economic and financial controls since the end of 1942. The adopted mechanism for achieving this hegemony, as Kolko explains in some detail, was a bilateral understanding with Britain which could then be presented to the world for multilateral rubber-stamping. As the policy developed, Churchill and Roosevelt accused each other of seeking exclusive concessions on the oil of the region; but American economic strength ensured that Ibn Saud's regime (in receipt of more Lend-Lease aid than he had any economic use for) fell into line in return for long-term assistance, decorously draped in the language of 'the improvement of economic conditions and living standards in Saudi Arabia'.[36]

But in Iran the obtrusive American presence – preoccupied with the elimination of British 'imperialism, monopoly and exploitation', in the words of Roosevelt's special representative Patrick Hurley – only succeeded in discrediting the compliant 'government' of Mohammed Saed which was faced with growing opposition from both nationalists and communists. None of this mattered until the Soviet Union staked its own claim for petroleum concessions in the five northern provinces of the country in September 1944. Though this was motivated by fear that Iran would otherwise become an American base along its borders, the Russian intervention

– which indirectly hastened the collapse of the Saed government and the rise of Mossadegh's nationalists – reminded the United States of Britain's utility in their common resistance to Soviet 'expansionism'. By December Washington agreed with the War Department that 'the continuance of the British Empire in some reasonable strength is in the strategic interests of the United States'.[37]

A timely demonstration of this truth was provided that very month when a British army was despatched to Greece, which had recently been liberated from Nazi occupation and was almost entirely controlled by ELAS, the communist-dominated Greek National Liberation Army.[38] In that 'naughty document', as he called it, which Churchill had handed to Stalin the previous October, Greece had been allotted to the British 'sphere of interest' with the dictator's blessing. The Russians accordingly kept silent as British forces intervened on the pretext of preventing a communist coup. In fact it was 'an intervention to crush the whole Greek resistance in order to restore the semi-colonial dependence of the past, an intervention carefully prepared at both the diplomatic and the military levels by Churchill since the summer of 1943 ... [as] part of a British policy for re-establishing the Empire and for the safeguarding of its communications'.[39] Roosevelt publicly refused to endorse the British action. It would take another year or so before the United States appreciated either the full extent of British economic weakness or the magnitude of the communist challenge to its plans for post-war hegemony. It was immediately apparent, however, that Churchill had the support of the Labour members of the War Cabinet.

# CHAPTER 5

# Social Imperialism Revisited, 1945–51

In the closing stages of the war it was already apparent that radical forces – nationalist and Leftist – would emerge stronger than ever before in most of the countries affected by the conflict. Greece provided one of the earliest indications of the British response to the new balance of forces and evidence of the fundamental continuity of policy between the incoming Labour government and the Churchill coalition. Soon after it took office it was evident that the Attlee administration fully approved of British intervention in Greece and was already taking steps elsewhere to repossess colonial territories that had been captured by the Japanese during the war. Indeed British actions in the Far East contributed to the restoration of French and Dutch colonialism as well, in accordance with war aims that were adopted in the wake of Japan's military successes. In part this was a question of closing ranks in the face of American talk of decolonisation and international trusteeships; but it was also informed by Britain's need for France as an ally in Europe. By the end of 1943 British officials had decided that the restoration of French control of Indo-China was necessary, even though they were well aware of Roosevelt's particular contempt for the record of colonialism in Southeast Asia.[1] Needless to say, there was no consideration of Vietnamese opinion when British policy was developed.

Local opposition to the return of the French was nevertheless deeply rooted and perfectly apparent to the British forces which entered the country in September 1945. Before the end of the month, however, they were implementing instructions to support the French by occupying Saigon until sufficient French troops were mobilised to take over from them. This policy of occupation was then extended so that the mainly Indian soldiers of the British command were required to take up positions throughout the south of the country. It rapidly brought the British into conflict with the provisional government of the Viet Minh. It also led to the rearming of Japanese soldiers – the late enemy – and the use of the Japanese air force in operations against the Vietnamese. By the end of the year French control of Saigon had been re-established, though the last British units remained in the country until April 1946. As John Saville points out, British public opinion knew little of all of this, partly because of the simultaneous British intervention in Indonesia on behalf of the Dutch – an intervention that received global publicity and provoked widespread opposition.[2]

One of the loudest boasts of the Labour government was that the old imperialism was dead, certainly so far as the British Commonwealth was concerned. But one of the crucial assumptions of its foreign policy was that Britain remained a power of the first rank, and the makers of this policy believed that its global role and possessions were the interdependent foundations of Great Power status. It will be noticed that the habit of appeasing the United States was never allowed to affect this perception of British interests and did not affect it now in the face of the challenge of American free trade imperialism. In fact the emergence during the war of a colonial development objective gave British imperialism a new gloss and self-confidence.

Yet the war had cost the country about a quarter of its wealth and left it dependent on the material support of the United States. Britain, in Keynes's words, was faced by 'a financial Dunkirk' in August 1945. President Truman (Roosevelt had died in April) abruptly announced the end of Lend-Lease on 21 August, just six days after the Japanese surrender. Yet the facts of Britain's feeble economic condition were clear enough. It had the largest external debt in history, and it was still mounting when Labour took office. Sterling liabilities stood at £3,500m and while exports earned just £350m, total outgoings including military expenditure abroad was running at the rate of £2,000m per annum. Even if the volume of imports could be kept at pre-war levels for the next three years, a 75 per cent increase in exports was required to correct the balance of payments deficit, given the loss of invisible earnings which was a legacy of the war. By the time that formidable increase could be achieved, it was estimated that an adverse balance of payments deficit of £1,250m would have accumulated – a sum that could only be covered by an American loan. To make matters worse, the only realistic source of supply for urgently needed imports of fuel, raw materials and food was the United States – a fact which underlined dependency on scarce dollars. Keynes eventually negotiated the required dollar loan in December 1945 (Congress ratified it in July 1946) but onerous conditions were attached requiring Britain to reduce the sterling balances (the external debt of £3,500m) and to make sterling convertible against the dollar within one year of the loan's Congressional approval.

The Foreign Office seems not to have noticed any of this, or at any rate blandly considered these problems to be temporary inconveniences only. Certainly, when Sir Orme Sargent – soon to become Permanent Under-Secretary – prepared his lengthy memorandum 'Stocktaking After VE Day' in July 1945, Britain's

economic enfeeblement was not allowed to constrain his view of
Britain's foreign interests and responsibilities. 'If we cease to regard
ourselves as a World Power', he argued, 'we shall gradually cease
to be one.' Thus in 'the immediate future', to avoid this distasteful
demotion, Sargent required Britain to 'take a stand' in Europe to
maintain its interests in Finland, Poland, Czechoslovakia, Austria,
Yugoslavia and Bulgaria and maintain 'close and friendly relations
with Italy, Greece, and Turkey'. In short, he insisted that 'in the
immediate future we must take the offensive in challenging
Communist penetration in as many of the Eastern countries of
Europe as possible'.[3]

Conflict between Britain and the Soviet Union had surfaced during
the war. At Yalta a commitment to free elections was included in
the Declaration on Liberated Europe, but by then Soviet domination
of Eastern Europe was a matter of fact and Churchill did not press
the issue – in part for want of US support. It will be recalled that
Churchill reached a 'percentages' agreement with Stalin in October
1944 dividing Eastern Europe into spheres of interest. Even on that
agreeable occasion, however, he was careful to insist – while
conceding Soviet domination in Bulgaria and Romania – that
Britain must remain the dominant power in the Mediterranean.
As the war drew to a close, tension between the erstwhile allies grew
as differences emerged over the future of Germany, the punishment
of war criminals, the question of reparations and the future of
Poland. The Allies began to remember things differently; the
'percentages agreement' had made no mention of Poland, the
Yalta conference had agreed to give Russian warships access to the
Mediterranean through the Dardanelles, while the Russians had
promised to hold free elections in Eastern Europe.

But in Britain all imperial strategists – with the exception, as we
shall see, of Attlee – were agreed that British control of the
Mediterranean was the *sine qua non* of imperial defence; this much
was clear. A Greek communist government was incompatible with
this, but so was Molotov's expressed interest in securing the Soviet
base in the Straits which the Russians considered their due. By the
summer of 1945 the Soviet desire for greater influence in the
eastern Mediterranean was enough to identify it as a threat to
British interests.[4] John Kent's research shows that it was this,
rather than Soviet policy in Eastern Europe, which conditioned
Foreign Office perceptions of the Soviet Union as an unfriendly
power and led to 'a policy of no deals or concessions of any kind
to the Soviet Union'.[5] Orme Sargent's perception in July 1945 of
the need for a diplomatic offensive to challenge Russia, even in
previously acceptable areas of Soviet domination such as Bulgaria,
was shared by other leading officials such as Gladwyn Jebb. For
their part, the Russians wanted free passage in the Straits and joint

Russian-Turkish bases to give them the same status at the eastern end of the Mediterranean as Britain enjoyed at Suez. These demands were tabled at the Potsdam summit in July 1945 and the Russians seemingly got their way when their claims were acknowledged by the new American President, Harry Truman.

The Foreign Office view was that any concession on this question would not only lead to Soviet domination in Greece and Turkey but, according to Gladwyn Jebb, 'to yield to any Russian demand would clearly mean that we were not prepared to play the part of a Great Power'.[6] The policy of no concessions was thus seen as essential for the defence of the British Empire and a demonstration of Britain's continuing potency. The reality was that Britain did not have the economic wherewithal to maintain a Great Power pose for very long. Keynes told Dalton in October 1945 that 'there is no way out remotely compatible with the present domestic policy of the Government except on the basis of substantial American aid'. But his warning was just as pertinent when applied to Britain's overseas commitments, which he tended to regard as evidence of *folie de grandeur*.[7] Clearly confrontation with the Soviet Union could only work if the United States aligned itself with British policy and provided the dollars to keep Britain afloat. But in Bevin, the Foreign Office had a man after its own heart. Before the Americans had committed themselves to confontation with Russia and before Britain had obtained the financial assistance it needed, Bevin was already at work convinced that Britain's Great Power status demanded the reinforcement of its military and economic role from one end of the Mediterranean to the other.

Thus when the future of the former Italian colonies was discussed at the London Council of Foreign Ministers in September 1945, Bevin's opening gambit was to oppose the American idea of a ten-year trusteeship over Libya and argue instead for British control of its eastern province of Cyrenaica where a military base would be established. Molotov actually agreed to this proposal, adding that the Russians were prepared to administer a ten-year trusteeship in neighbouring Tripolitania where they would develop a port for their merchant fleet. But in the interests of excluding the Russians from the region altogether, Bevin changed his mind, proposing that an international trusteeship represented a better alternative after all, just as the Americans had insisted. The talks broke down at this point but Molotov accused Bevin of 'trying to create a monopoly in the Mediterranean' when the two met at the Soviet embassy on 1 October. Bevin simply replied that Britain could not tolerate a 'new military power ... across the lifeline of the British Empire'.[8] It was better, according to the Foreign Secretary, that Tripolitania and Cyrenaica should be regarded as 'an international region'. Meanwhile the British had also decided that Italian Somaliland,

British Somaliland and the Ogaden should come under a single trusteeship with Britain as trustee, but for tactical reasons the proposal was not tabled until the Paris meeting of the Council of Foreign Ministers in April 1946.

In reality the Foreign Office did not like the American proposal for international trusteeships. Britain claimed 'special strategic rights' in Libya, derived, according to Foreign Office logic, from its role in North East Africa since the eighteenth century. But conscious that this argument might not convince the Americans, officials decided that Britain should propose the rapid independence of Cyrenaica so that, in the words of one of them, 'we can conclude with her an alliance such as we have had with Egypt' – a reference to the hated treaty of 1936 which the Egyptian government was determined to abrogate.[9] British confidence about the benefits that would accrue from such an arrangement was based on the Foreign Office's special relationship with Sheikh Idris, the Emir of the Senussi, and a local collaborator of the sort that could no longer be found so easily in Egypt. Officials even toyed with the idea that the Senussi writ might be extended over Tripolitania. The problem was mulled over in the first weeks of 1946. General Smuts even had his say, depicting the Balkan states as 'virtual Soviet satellites' with Russia extending outwards from the Adriatic to the Straits, casting greedy eyes on 'the Persian Gulf with all its oil and other values', across 'a weakened and dependent Iran'. It was clear to him – and Bevin made known his concurrence – that the contemplated arrangements for the dispersal of the former Italian colonies threatened Britain's status as a Great Power since any international trusteeship administration in which Russia could claim a major say 'might place her in a commanding position in the Mediterranean'.[10]

An interdepartmental committee reported on the issue in detail in February 1946, taking the same line as Smuts. It particularly disliked the American proposal for five-power advisory committees to supervise the UN trusteeship of Libya because it would give the Russians a say in the area. As for the idea that a referendum should be held to test local opinion on the future of the country, it was regarded as frankly ludicrous. Press reports in Cairo were quick to pick up British obstruction of US plans, however, and according to General Paget, the Commander-in-Chief in the Middle East, 'have [had] a most disturbing effect on the already tense situation in Libya' itself. Paget was particularly concerned that the British government should be seen to support a referendum in the country in accordance with Article 76(b) of the UN Charter. Officials were sceptical, noting that referenda did not always work well even in 'civilised' countries like Switzerland.[11]

The Chiefs of Staff naturally insisted that a Russian presence in North Africa could only 'lower our prestige and lead to unrest among the Arab tribes' – oblivious in their usual way to the existing unrest caused by the British presence. Bevin went to the Council of Foreign Ministers in Paris (25 April–16 May 1946) determined to neutralise the Russians by proposing immediate independence for Cyrenaica and Tripolitania, after due consultation with the inhabitants. He explained that all this was in accordance with 'solemn pledges' which the British had made to the Senussi in 1941 in return for their assistance in the war. Molotov's proposals – first for collective trusteeships, later for Italian trusteeship over the whole of Libya – were both opposed by the Foreign Secretary. When the Americans came round to the idea that the Italians should resume control, Bevin changed tack again. 'Cyrenaica was vital from the point of view of the British Empire', he avowed. This implicitly acknowledged the truth in Molotov's assertion that the British had only proposed independence for Libya the better to keep armed forces there, just as they had long succeeded in doing in Egypt – an 'independent' member of the UN, currently demanding British withdrawal. The British, according to Molotov, 'wanted all of the Italian colonies and a bit of Ethiopia as well'. As late as February 1948 Bevin was still advising the Cabinet as to the desirability of a UK trusteeship of the whole of Libya, observing that the Chiefs of Staff would not oppose an Italian claim on Somaliland and Eritrea as compensation for its loss.[12]

The debate about the future of the Italian colonies shows quite clearly that British policy was constructed on the assumption that Britain, as a Great Power, could only retain this status by defending – and even extending – its global interests. This meant a measure of conflict with the United States – a conflict well established by the end of the war – and confrontation with the Soviet Union, since the latter was intent on establishing its 'right' to a role in the Mediterranean commensurate with its membership of the 'Big Three' and thereby threatening the imperial 'lifeline', according to the Foreign Office. After the complete destruction of Germany, moreover, the Soviet Union was necessarily the main problem in Europe from the British point of view. What was needed here was a balance of power that would enable Britain to concentrate on its main overseas interests. On both counts this could only be achieved by involving the United States, the source of Britain's financial support and the only Power capable of checking the Russians.

As Keynes cautioned ministers on the urgent need for American aid in the autumn of 1945, Bevin was already (23 September) telling Molotov 'that it seemed to him that [Britain's] relationship with the Russians about the whole European problem was drifting into the same condition as that which we had found ourselves in with

Hitler'.[13] Molotov may have reflected that it had taken previous foreign secretaries over six years to reach a final conclusion over Hitler, but not much more than six weeks for this one to reach the point of belligerence. Yet the evidence concerning Soviet ambitions and capacities was, to say the least, far more ambiguous than Hitler's had ever been. The Soviet Union had just been on the receiving end of the 'most monstrous war of conquest, enslavement and extermination in modern times', in the words of Jurgen Forster, and had emerged with a burden of costs which Susan Linz estimates as 'the equivalent of eighteen to twenty-five years' earnings, or work effort, of the 1945 labour force'.[14] While the full extent of the disaster was not known – Stalin concealed the true figure for fatalities, for example, and wreaked his own havoc on the country when the war was over – it was clear enough that the European regions of the Soviet Union had been devastated. But the knowledge of this and the fact of rapid demobilisation of the Red Army did not affect the British perception of Soviet expansionism.

Stalin's complicity in Britain's war against the Greek Left, and communist collaboration in the disarming of the French and Italian resistance movements, could not affect the issue either. Although these actions provided evidence that the Russians were honouring at least some of their wartime agreements on discrete spheres of influence,[15] a communist threat existed nonetheless. It existed in the shape of the Russian demand for implementation of the Yalta promise to give their warships greater access to the Mediterranean via the Dardenelles; in the fact of Soviet domination of Eastern Europe and its opposition to both the revival of Germany and an independent Poland; in the form of communist parties with growing popular support in Europe and Asia. As early as September 1945 Bevin construed Soviet demands for a Mediterranean port in Tripolitania as 'no less than a bid for the mineral resources of tropical Africa'.[16] He saw ulterior motives in Russian support for a Jewish homeland in Palestine; the immigration of 'sufficient indoctrinated Jews' would, he believed, turn Palestine into a communist state. The Foreign Office advised the Americans accordingly, demonstrating that this was something more than the fantasy of one man.[17] In Cyprus, Iran and Iraq, officials talked of the danger of communism, should British policy fail.[18] The imperial dimension of the communist threat was plain enough. As Furedi shows, Soviet denunciations of racism and imperialism 'found widespread resonance among anti-colonial activists' and put Britain on the defensive. In October 1946 one Foreign Office official admitted that British problems in the Middle East, though 'not created by Russia', were 'deliberately aggravated by a savage Soviet campaign of anti-British propaganda'.[19]

Even as late as this, however, the Foreign Office had to contend with American anti-colonialism as well. In November 1946 officials even wondered whether 'the contemptuous ignorance shown by the United States incites the Far East propagandists to greater excesses than does Russian opposition'.[20] Such doubts serve to underline the point made earlier that as Bevin embarked on his policy of confrontation with the Soviet Union and consolidation of Britain's imperial interests in the autumn of 1945, American financial and political support was far from being assured. The US State Department believed that Britain had got off lightly at Bretton Woods. The privileged access of imperial countries to their colonies was to have been eliminated; Britain was to be prised out of the sterling bloc; and yet on both matters only promises of future consideration could be extracted. But when Keynes negotiated the urgently needed dollar loan in December 1945, the Americans got closer to their goal of eliminating 'foreign exchange restrictions which hamper the growth of world trade' by insisting on the convertibility of sterling within one year of Congressional approval of the loan. The US Secretary to the Treasury called this 'the most important purpose' of the loan from the American standpoint.[21]

Britain was also finally forced to agree to the abolition of discriminatory import quotas and by the time the General Agreement on Tariffs and Trade (GATT) was signed in the spring of 1947, it had eliminated around 5 per cent of its trade formerly subject to imperial preference. American policy also led, in 1946, to the collapse of the pre-war production and marketing arrangements between British and US oil companies for Middle Eastern oil; 'a vigorous fight for post-war concessions, with no holds barred' had raged during the war[22] and the American share of the region's oil output rose from 16 per cent in 1939 to 31 per cent in 1946 and 60 per cent by 1953. The evidence was all around that the US was intent on prising open the trading area based on sterling – the biggest trading area in the world. America's own dependence on an open world economy made this imperative.

But it would also serve no useful American purpose to enfeeble Britain in the process; Britain needed to be strong enough to play a constructive role in financing and removing barriers to European trade and this required confidence in sterling and the restoration of the City's role as a financial centre. The United States was thus engaged in a contradictory process of taking advantage of Britain's economic weaknesses while depending on Britain's ability to assist it in the construction of a liberal economic order. Thus the Americans favoured writing off much of Britain's international debt – the sterling balances – both because a debt that exceeded Britain's reserves was incompatible with a strong pound and also because its continued existence would bias the holders of the debt to purchase British, rather than American, goods.

It was also noticed in Britain that Congressional approval for the $3.75b loan negotiated by Keynes was greatly encouraged by the anti-communist speeches of Senator Vandenberg and Representative McCormack in July 1945.[23] In November Britain's ambassador to Washington, Lord Halifax, observed that there was 'a well-established principle that our stocks appreciate as those of the Soviet Union decline and vice versa'.[24] This principle was not lost on the Foreign Office (indeed Orme Sargent had anticipated it back in July) which had every reason to play-up the communist problem; but as Halifax indicated, at least some Americans already took the same view. As early as the autumn of 1944, in fact, George Kennan, Averell Harriman's chief adviser in Moscow, cautioned Washington on the need 'to determine in conjunction with the British the line beyond which we cannot afford to permit the Russians to exercise unchallenged power'.[25] The Foreign Office could not have put it better – a partnership along such lines was exactly what British foreign policy hoped to bring about.

American strategists warned Truman just days after he assumed the presidency that Russia would 'emerge ... as by far the strongest nation in Europe and Asia ... if the United States should stand aside'.[26] The Polish question began to rise up the American agenda and by the end of 1945 it was linked to the existence of strongly pro-Soviet governments in Bulgaria and Romania and the intensification of the Russian campaign for a base in the Dardennelles, with Stalin applying diplomatic pressure and military intimidation against Turkey. Soviet power in the region was apparently rising, as an uprising in northern Iran in the autumn testified; a pro-Soviet regime was established which immediately gave the Russians oil-drilling rights.

British influence, on the other hand, was almost everywhere in trouble in the Middle East when the war ended. Yet it was determined to remain the foremost military power in the entire region, the prospective loss of India only serving to amplify the insistence of the strategists on this point, if not the cogency of their arguments. Oil was undoubtedly a key factor, as the scramble for oil rights between Britain and the United States testifies; later the Chiefs of Staff added the argument that the British presence would entail the possession of bases from which Russia's own oil fields could be bombed. Since the end of the war the American government had been cognisant of the fact that Middle Eastern oil reserves were equal to three-quarters of the known US reserves. America's very evident determination to control this asset meant that it would not take much to convince its leaders, as Britain's were already convinced, that Russia was 'malevolently bent on expansion southwards' into these preserves.[27]

British policies had, however, contributed enormously to its insecurity of tenure. In Egypt there was determination to abrogate the 1936 treaty, and rid the country of at least 150,000 British troops. A similarly massive military presence in Palestine was equally to no avail and damaging to the all-important 'prestige' of Britain in the region. Worse still, the oligarchs of the Muslim world, the traditional collaborators, were faced with serious nationalist agitation in a number of countries. For example, Britain's assistance in the repression of Kurdish nationalist agitation in Iraq after 1943 – a repeat performance of the coercion of 1931–32 when the RAF and the Iraqi army worked together on the task – succeeded in pushing the nationalists towards communism and it was the Iraqi communists who rallied to the defence of the Kurds in September 1945 during another wave of government repression.[28] Britain supported a corrupt and crisis-torn regime which was only kept in power by repression and election-rigging throughout the 1940s. Oil and the utility of airforce bases within striking distance of the Soviet Union were the incentives which interested the Foreign Office; the poverty of the mass of the population was simply ignored until mounting popular discontent peaked in the late 1950s.

A similar policy operated in Iran where the communists had also made progress as the Tudeh Party established a genuinely country-wide base. As we have seen, the Soviet Union acted to support the creation of two autonomous governments in Iran's northern province of Azerbaijan; the north-western of these, neighbouring Iraq, became an independent Kurdish state. In all probability neither of these states could have been formed without the presence of the Soviet occupying forces which originated in the Anglo-Soviet invasion of 1941, but nor did they immediately collapse when the Russians withdrew. The truth is that Iran, just like Iraq, had been subject to considerable political instability, economic dislocation and social unrest ever since the invasion of 1941. Britain's 'contemptuous attitude towards the Iranian ruling class' and its determination to retain the central and southern provinces to suit its own economic interests contributed to the unrest when the war was over. The Anglo-Iranian Oil Company – in which the British government held a controlling interest – had exercised 'considerable control over Iranian affairs'; its refinery at Abadan was the largest in the world and by 1945 Iran was producing more oil than the rest of the Arab world combined.[29] The greed of the Anglo-Iranian Company is illustrated by the fact that between 1945 and 1950 it paid more in taxes to the British government on its $1.125b profit than it paid in 'royalties' to the Iranian government. But from the moment US troops and advisers entered the country in 1942 to facilitate Lend-Lease shipments to Russia, the Americans worked towards securing Iranian independence from both Britain and Russia, the better to establish its own dominance. Under American protection the Iranian government was now 'free' to invite the United States to bid for the southern oil concession, which it did in the autumn of 1944. This prompted the Soviet Union, however, to put in a claim for exploitation rights in the north of the country; further discussions were then postponed until the end of the war.

The persistence of Russian demands for oil concessions combined with 'the wide popular support of the Tudeh Party'[30] and the existence of the pro-Soviet republics in Azerbaijan and Kurdistan ensured that the Anglo-American struggle for control of Iranian oil became less important than the exclusion of the Soviet Union, but not before the British proposed to formalise the British and Soviet spheres of influence at the Moscow Council of Foreign Ministers in December 1945. This attempt to consolidate the British position, even at the cost of a concession to Russia, was abandoned in the face of American opposition. From this point, as Kolko observes, 'the only thing that bound the United States and the United Kingdom together was a mutual fear of Russia and the Left in the postwar world and the necessity of fighting a common enemy on the same front'.[31] Although Truman had acknowledged Russia's claim on rights of access to the Mediterranean at Potsdam in July 1945, by January 1946 he was accusing it of planning an invasion of Turkey and seizure of the Black Sea Straits. Stalin greatly added to such fears by refusing to withdraw Soviet troops from Iran in March 1946, under the terms of a wartime agreement which both Britain and the United States complied with. The spectre of Soviet control through the Balkans to Turkey and Iran strengthened the argument that the Russians were ideologically driven to world domination. March was the month of Churchill's Fulton speech, with its warning of an imperilled 'Christian civilisation' in all countries outside America and the British Empire. It was also the month when the Joint Chiefs of Staff at the Pentagon concluded that 'the defeat or disintegration of the British Empire would eliminate from Eurasia the last bulwark of resistance between the US and Soviet expansion ... Militarily, our present position as a world power is of necessity closely interwoven with that of Great Britain.'[32]

This view came to prevail in spite of the withdrawal of Soviet troops from Iran in April 1946 and the general trend of the Red Army's rapid demobilisation from twelve to three million men by 1948. The developing Cold War must also have been a factor in Attlee's eventual capitulation in the face of persistent Foreign Office and miltary pressure to maintain Britain's traditional hegemony in the Middle East. Attlee had favoured international control of the Suez Canal, questioned the economic burdens involved in continuing the imperial role and observed that from the Russian point of view a country like Egypt was simply a British satellite. He was initially opposed to the acquisition of Cyrenaica and also noted that the strategic argument for a British presence in the Middle East was obsolete now that air-power had revolutionised defence. From the spring of 1945 until January 1947 he fought this rearguard action against the Foreign Office, Bevin and the military. The chorus opposing Attlee prevailed, of course, with its insistence that the Middle East was a vital strategic and economic asset to Britain and that any withdrawal would simply create a vacuum into which would step the Russians en route southward into Africa.[33]

Africa's economic value to Britain had been amply demonstrated during the war, but post-war conditions served to emphasise it much further. Britain was dependent on imported food, fuel and raw materials without having the dollars to buy them from the United States. The dollar shortage was universal and widely believed to be permanent, while Europe as a whole was unable to feed itself and faced the exhaustion of many of its raw materials in the context of worsening terms of trade.[34] The recurring expectation of a slump in the US economy underlined the perceived need to restore the British economy to an independent footing.[35] The huge external debt in the shape of the sterling balances was just under £3,500m – over five times the size of Britain's gold and dollar reserves, and rising. This debt, it was pointed out in 1946, represented a claim on Britain's resources equivalent to one-seventh of its annual net national income, a claim it was in no position to satisfy.[36] Of the total, £454m was owed to Crown Colonies, over which it was possible for London to exert stringent controls. The result was that this portion of the debt rose to £928m by 1951, while some of the countries concerned made export earnings which they were forbidden to spend in dollar markets or in Britain itself.

Thus the circumstances of Britain's economic plight increased its need for cheap imports from within the sterling area and highlighted the necessity for markets capable of absorbing the massive (75 per cent) export expansion that it required. The captive colonial economies could be useful on both counts, but only if they were developed. As early as May 1943 officials had toyed with the idea that the colonial sterling assets could be used for this purpose.[37] When Labour came into power, however, the overriding need to make dollar earnings and protect Britain's parlous reserves foreclosed this option. Nothing could be allowed to increase the purchasing power of the colonies. Indeed, the Treasury wanted the debt cancelled but ultimately accepted the Colonial Office proposal that long-term, interest-free loans could substitute for outright cancellation. The war-inspired system of forced borrowing thus continued to prevail with the result that the colonial sterling balances more than doubled in the lifetime of the Labour government. So despite the undoubted need for colonial development and the very great volume of ministerial talk about it, capital that might have been used for development purposes was actually drained out of the colonies during these years.

The capital outflow from Labour Britain was admittedly vast – equivalent to 8 per cent of national income and nearly equal to net domestic capital formation in 1947 alone.[38] But the white Dominions received the bulk of it, especially Australia and South Africa (gold mines). In the colonies there was net disinvestment. This point needs repeating because Labour's colonial policies are widely misunderstood. The standard work on the Attlee governments, for example, complacently argues that 'in general, the requirements of the mother country and of the developing territories under British rule seemed to flow in the same beneficent direction'.[39] While conceding that 'social imperialism on the grand "Round Table" model was pursued relentlessly, from Jamaica to Tanganyika', Kenneth Morgan reinforces this favourable view by describing its practitioners as 'ragged-trousered philanthropists'.[40] This confuses the no doubt sincere desire of reformers like Creech Jones and Rita Hinden 'for a positive colonial policy, based on long-term economic, technological, and educational development', as Morgan puts it, with the reality, which was very different. 'The basic fact', according to D.K. Fieldhouse, 'is that between 1945 and 1951 Britain exploited those dependencies that were politically unable to defend their own interests in more ways and with more serious consequences than at any time since the overseas colonies were established.'[41]

Clearly, some of this exploitation required Britain to undertake colonial development – though not all of it, as the frozen sterling balances attest. But it is an elementary fact that development in a region does not invariably amount to development of a region. It was precisely the long-term infrastructural development desired by Bevin in the Middle East and by Creech Jones in Africa that was precluded by shortages of every conceivable item relevant to such projects in Britain itself; and as we have seen colonies that were net dollar earners were not allowed to help themselves by purchasing equipment in the United States. Even if they had been so allowed they could never have commanded the resources required to realise the fantastic ideas which Labour ministers countenanced, such as the purchase of popular allegiance to Britain in the Middle East and India and the nullification of nationalist sentiment. Relatively modest amounts of capital were found to fund specific projects – the ill-conceived groundnuts scheme in Tanganyika (costing £40m) being the best known example. Just £8m flowed annually from

Britain to the Commonwealth between 1946 and 1951 under the terms of the Colonial Development and Welfare Act. But much more (£86m between 1945 and 1949) was found in government grants and loans to rehabilitate the rubber and tin industries of Malaya since these commodities were respectively the second and fifth biggest dollar earners in the sterling area and the government's real priority was to overcome the dollar gap.[42] In 1948 British forces began a prolonged military campaign against communist insurgents to protect its control of these resources.

While net dollar earners such as Malaya, Northern Rhodesia and the Gold Coast were unable to spend hard currency outside the sterling area, Britain itself prioritised exports to dollar markets. Shortages of every kind afflicted the colonial economies and the resulting inflation fuelled popular unrest, as in the Nigerian general strike of 1945 and the dock strikes in Mombasa and Dar-es-Salaam in 1947. Under the sterling colonial exchange standard, to which the dependencies were tied, the policy of forced borrowing had another arm: colonies were required to hold 100 per cent cover for their currencies in London with the result that funds that might have been used for investment actually provided Britain with cheap credit. British control of these subordinate monetary systems also had the advantage, when Britain was forced in 1949 to devalue the pound against the dollar by a third of its value, of enabling the government to devalue the colonial currencies by the same amount and thus reduce the real burden of the blocked sterling balances.

The physical controls on colonial commerce introduced during the war – such as bulk-buying by government agencies at prices set in London – was continued via a system of marketing boards established within the colonies in 1945. These boards had monopsonist powers to purchase the main African export crops and the gap between world prices and the price paid to producers widened. Whereas colonial governments had retained the difference during the war to help finance the war effort, the post-war surplus eventually found its way into development schemes in the 1950s. What the African labourer and farmer received in the first instance, however, was tax rises and a continuation of the production drives instigated during the war. Africans were neither consulted about these plans, nor seen as particularly competent in the fulfilment of them.[43] No doubt this was one reason why Labour actively encouraged the departure of 8,000 white immigrants to Kenya between 1945 and 1948, where the reactionary Governor, Sir Philip Mitchell, was an enthusiast for the new Fabian doctrine proclaiming the necessity of economic development as a necessary prelude to political advance. Mitchell, incidentally, was also of the opinion that Africans were not yet in 'a state of spiritual, moral, social, cultural, and economic development' capable of democracy.[44]

The white monopoly of the best land in Kenya persisted without government interference, though attempts by Africans to obtain control of profitable schemes was just as surely resisted as were the efforts of the East African TUC to obtain official recognition.

The leading role of the settlers in Kenya was felt all the more to be 'unchallangeable' in the context of the new technocratic drive for increased economic output. But the influx of Europeans was not confined to Kenya; a body of experts, officials and settlers arrived throughout East Africa. In Tanganyika – which Britain reluctantly placed under a United Nations trusteeship in January 1946, its own toothless version of trusteeship having been rejected at San Francisco the year previously – agricultural development involved compulsion to grow crops which Africans perceived as designed to address the post-war European food crisis rather than their own interests. In Uganda the producers of cotton and coffee, obliged to sell under bulk-buying agreements at artificially low prices, paid export taxes amounting to 50 per cent in the years 1948–52. They were faced, furthermore, with processing industries which were in effect 'given monopoly status and profits [that were] excessively high. Since the firms in them were at the beginning of the period entirely non-African and throughout the period substantially so, economic conflict was aggravated by racial feeling.'[45] It could hardly be otherwise. Colonial governments, having bent things to assist the British war effort for six years, were now bending them to subsidise British reconstruction. It amounted to 'a second colonial occupation'.[46]

Labour ministers – tinged, as avowed socialists, with a vague anti-imperialist aura – were of course at pains to ditch the unacceptable face of Empire and a substantial amount of rhetoric was devoted to this task. The language of development undoubtedly assisted this process but in the end the Cold War was probably decisive. Most of the more articulate and untainted (non-communist) critics of Labour's foreign policy capitulated after the Americans finally saw that their self-interest was bound up with the economic restoration of Western Europe. The Marshall Plan or European Recovery Programme, announced in June 1947, allowed Labour to remain faithful to its reform programme at home and maintain Britain's ruinously expensive world role – a feat otherwise impossible to sustain. It also sealed the Cold War, when the Soviet Union rejected the terms of the Marshall Plan both for itself and for its East European satellites. Under these circumstances, leading Labour left-wingers, who had recently predicted and warned against just such a polarisation of international relations, were transformed into supporters of government policy. *Tribune*, erstwhile conscience of the party, joined in the 'development' chorus, offering its own advice on the need to stand firm in the colonies and resist the 'Communist bandits'.[47] More to the point, the only power capable of dismantling the Empire – the United States – had definitively discovered that it had no interest in doing so.

American pressure had nevertheless already contributed to Britain's disengagement from India, the one big piece of evidence for those who believe that Labour was interested in decolonisation. Closer inspection of the evidence, however, does not suggest that this was an automatic effect of the Labour victory. The scheme seriously considered by the Cabinet in 1942 to 'engage in a grand scheme of majestic politics involving direct appeals to Indian peasants and workers over the heads of an "unrepresentative" bourgeois Congress'[48] survived for a time under the new dispensation. When that was dropped 'the Viceroy [Lord Wavell] and London toyed with the idea of a further round of repression to force Congress into a reasonable frame of mind', but this idea was rejected just as quickly.[49] Bevin, however, was still complaining of a 'defeatist attitude' and a policy of 'scuttle' in January 1947, but was silenced when Attlee asked for 'a practical alternative'.[50] Britain did not have the divisions to govern India by force, even if it had had the will to do so, which would have involved defying international opinion as well as contradicting the mass of British promises and concessions accumulated since the First World War. What it did expect to get was something like the settlement proposed by the Cripps Mission in 1942: the retention of a federal India within the Commonwealth, Indian reliance on British military leadership, Indian military support and facilities for British operations in Southeast Asia, and India's continued membership of the sterling area. Most of these hopes were dashed by the time Bevin was complaining of scuttle and Labour did not get the settlement it wanted. A hasty, improvised withdrawal was carried out not dissimilar to the retreat from Palestine a year later and in acknowledgement of the same problem of ungovernability.

Once the loss of India was seen to be inevitable, the Labour government became even more dedicated to the development of the Middle East and Africa as its replacements, though this contradicted the original rationale for the Middle Eastern empire which was precisely to defend India.[51] Now, however, the argument was that it was essential to hold this 'gateway' to Africa and the Indian Ocean against the communists; that it was the basis for British prestige in the whole of Southern Europe, the Balkans and Turkey; that, according to Bevin, it was of enormous economic value to Britain. The Canal Zone and Palestine in particular were looked upon as a gigantic British military preserve. The scale of the commitment in the region was vast; as late as the spring of 1948 about 270,000 British troops were stationed in a dozen different territories in the area – and this at a time of an acute 'manpower shortage' in British industry (estimated since 1946 at one million

workers).[52] Advice from the Chiefs of Staff and Foreign Office –
equally disinterested in Britain's economic condition and of Arab
national sentiment – was adamant that the region was a vital
'strategic reserve' into which the Russians would inevitably move
should Britain withdraw.

Yet Britain also had military commitments in Germany, Trieste,
Austria and Greece; it kept navies in the Pacific and Caribbean,
the Mediterranean and the Indian Ocean. At the end of 1946 the
armed forces were 1,427,000 strong, yet that autumn it had been
found necessary to decide in favour of peacetime conscription
which was introduced in 1947. The cost of the armed services in
1946–47 proved to be 15 per cent of gross national product and
it was still as high as 7 per cent in 1948. About half of this cost was
absorbed by Britain's imperial commitments, including new ones
such as the 20,000-strong garrison in Cyrenaica and costly operations
such as the Malayan Emergency, where imperial interests and
Cold War objectives coincided. Indeed the Cold War in the Far
and Middle East was by now the chief justification for the
maintenance of a global role which Britain could not afford. Barnett
estimates that the straightforward financial cost alone in 1946–50
of maintaining armed forces demanded by the world role, as distinct
from those needed for Britain's own defence, was £300–400m per
annum – an amount equivalent to the total annual capital investment
of those years in manufacturing industry other than iron and steel.[53]

It will seem ironic that Bevin, one of the chief advocates of the
world role, frequently made known his concern to 'prevent a
deteriorating standard of life' in Britain. But for the Foreign
Secretary the British standard of living depended on Empire and
was intimately related to his preoccupation with imperial
development, as he made clear in a memo to Attlee in July 1947.[54]
In this communication he talked of his anxiety to establish an
economic independence vis-a-vis the United States by means of
colonial development. Work was begun on drawing up an inventory
of raw materials scarce in the United States but capable of expanded
colonial production. The Colonial Sub-Committee of the European
Reconstruction Committee found these to include tin (Malaya
and Nigeria), copper (Northern Rhodesia), bauxite (British Guiana),
asbestos and chrome ore (Southern Rhodesia), manganese (Gold
Coast), industrial diamonds (Gold Coast, Sierra Leone and South
West Africa), graphite (Ceylon), vanadium (South West Africa and
Northern Rhodesia) and cadmium (South West Africa). Creech
Jones observed during these discussions that the work was already
in hand, though it was hampered by 'all-pervading shortages'; he
also commented that 'it may pay us to see that colonial producers
get the highest possible price', in other words the market price.[55]

In June a Colonial Primary Products Committee was set up 'to review, commodity by commodity, the possibility of increasing colonial production'.

A year later 'major success' was reported in 'the Colonial export drive' with two-thirds of commodities demonstrating increased volume in 1947 as compared with 1946, and colonial dollar earnings running at $600–700m in the first half of 1948. At the same time expenditure in the colonies was 'curtailed', in spite of higher prices, thanks to 'a system of dollar ceilings'. The colonial contribution to UK imports had risen from 5.4 per cent in 1938 to 10.2 per cent in the first half of 1948 and had resulted in a 'considerable saving of dollars'. Moreover, colonial produce such as tin, rubber, cocoa, oil seeds and sisal had been important in 'the successful negotiation of bi-lateral trade agreements, for example, with European countries for increased supplied [sic] of foodstuffs for the UK'. Finally, the report mentioned the growth in public revenues of colonial governments, and the accumulation of special funds from these resources, held on account in London, which could finance future development; Ugandan cotton and coffee, West Indies sugar and West African sugar and oilseeds accounted for £81m of these reserves by September 1948.[56] This was no doubt all very gratifying, though no basis for Bevin's wilder imaginings such as the conviction, expressed in Cabinet in 1948, that the development of Africa would make the United States 'dependent on us and eating out of our hand in four or five years'.

In fact Bevin had been genuinely concerned to establish Britain's economic and political independence from the United States since he first became Foreign Secretary and envisaged success in this regard with the emergence of Western Europe as a 'third force'. The scheme he had in mind was West European economic restoration on the basis of coordinated development of the region's colonial possessions, particularly those in Africa. From the summer of 1946 he had investigated the possibility of a customs union with France on this imperial basis. As he told the French Prime Minister, Renadier, in September 1947, 'with their populations of 47 million and 40 million respectively and with their vast colonial possessions they could, if they acted together, be as powerful as either the Soviet Union or the United States'. Bevin was particularly concerned to stress that 'they possessed between them supplies of raw materials greater than those of any other country' and that he was impressed 'by the number of raw materials in which the United States was lacking'.[57] Various committees were established to promote this coordination which was expanded to involve the Belgians, Dutch and South Africans, with Bevin calling for the involvement of Portugal and Italy as well. Africa was the particular focus for 'development' and it was made clear from the start that West

European economic integration was 'wanted for political reasons, such as the combatting of communism', as well as to secure its future economic independence.[58] Once the division of Europe was seen as 'inevitable', Bevin and his officials saw the Marshall Plan as an 'opportunity' to move towards the economic integration of its Western nations in a customs union that would promote 'a union ... which would have natural cohesion and political reality'.[59]

Having overcome its fears of regional blocs obstructing multilateral trade, the United States was determined to promote the economic integration of Western Europe as a measure for the restoration of capitalism and the defeat of communism. On the eve of the Marshall Plan, Western Europe was still well short of pre-war industrial and agricultural production levels (88 and 83 per cent respectively), despite having already received some $9b in various aid programmes.[60] The American policy-makers reasoned that all the barriers to trade would have to come down to create a market in Western Europe analogous to their own. It was thus decided that Marshall aid should be conditional on the economic cooperation of the Europeans themselves and the British recognised that effort in this direction was necessary to sell the European recovery programme to Congress. But they were just as quick to see that it could conflict with imperial interests and the development of colonial resources which were regarded as 'vital for our long-term viability', in the words of a memorandum prepared for the Cabinet Economic Policy Committee.[61]

Ever since the Cabinet's first considerations of a customs union, it was clear that the government wanted nothing to do with any scheme that would compromise Britain's economic ties with the Empire–Commonwealth, with which it did twice as much trade as with Western Europe. The 'world-power complex' was even more important in influencing this judgement. At the International Trade Organisation negotiations in Geneva in June 1947, for example, Bevin told the American negotiators that Britain 'was not just another European country'; 'through the resources of its empire ... it could make a contribution to European recovery second only to that of the United States'.[62]

The Treasury and the Colonial Office were at one in seeing European union as a threat to Britain's preferential trading advantage and the preservation of the sterling area. An interdepartmental working committee, set up in September 1947, warned that a customs union would inevitably evolve a supranational authority and Commonwealth ties would weaken. In November Bevin repeated to the Cabinet Economic Policy Committee his conviction that 'some measure of economic unity' was essential to establish Western Europe's independence from the United States. But he also emphasised that European control 'over important Colonial territories' was vital to the project since they contained 'resources [which] would be available to sustain this new structure of economic cooperation'. Cripps agreed that 'the first step should be the creation of a Customs Union with the Colonial Empire' and even Dalton – a man whose diary talks of 'pullulating, poverty-stricken, diseased nigger communities' – said that 'the principal value of any arrangement we might enter into with Western Europe lay in the Colonial resources which this might make available to us'. Harold Wilson spoke against a customs union but added, no doubt superfluously, 'that it would be inadvisable to appear lukewarm or hostile' to the proposal in view of American support for the idea. In discussion the following point was made:

> The United States and Russia would be critical of any arrangements which appeared to involve the exploitation of Colonial areas in the interests of Western Europe, or any restrictions on the development of multilateral trading. It would therefore be inadvisable in any public statement to lay emphasis on the inclusion of Colonial territories within any arrangements that might be contemplated.[63]

In the months since Bevin first prompted investigation into the economic pros and cons of a customs union with France in the summer of 1946, officials had given the subject of European economic integration enough consideration to be perfectly aware of the implications for Britain of its exclusion from the sort of project favoured by the Americans. Some departments, for example, warned that even in the short run there would be 'devastating competition from the Continent' in certain basic industries such as steel and chemicals. Some officials saw that if Britain stood alone 'we shall just manage to survive as pigmies between two giants', always dependent on one of them for protection. Robin Hankey (head of the Northern Department at the Foreign Office) observed that 'we have not had, in practice, sufficient industry to arm the British Empire for the last twenty-five years and in two wars ... we have only survived because the Americans have made the arms for us and in effect given us the money to pay for them'. Gladwyn Jebb talked of 'the dismal choice' of Soviet satellite or poor dependant of the United States which awaited an isolated Britain, but also reasoned that 'a Customs Union does not make sense unless it leads on to economic and political union'; this meant losing the Empire and contemplating the eventual German domination of Western Europe in perhaps 20 years time.

Nevertheless, it was also pointed out in discussion that 'every long-term economic and strategic argument would seem to be in favour ... economic integration would surely offer greater security and stability than any system of military alliances could achieve'.

Hankey argued that 'Western Europe as a whole ... is potentially a Great Power even by modern standards'. But he went on to outline the course of action which Bevin championed in Cabinet: 'we can, I believe, only meet this situation by actively building up the economic potential of the Empire, and by pressing forward the economic and political reconstruction of Western Europe and also coordinating its defence as a whole'.[64] A month after this official brain-storming session, the Foreign Secretary won general support in Cabinet for his proposal that steps should be taken to 'consolidate the forces of Western European countries and their colonial possessions'. As Bevin argued, 'some closer form of union should be created in Western Europe in order to resist the increasing penetration of Soviet influence'. It would, however, be 'necessary to mobilise the resources of Africa in support of any Western European union ... if some such union could be created, including not only the countries of Western Europe but also their colonial possessions in Africa and the East this would form a bloc which, in both population and productive capacity, could stand on an equality with the western hemisphere and Soviet blocs'.[65]

It took until the autumn of 1949 before Bevin reluctantly acknowledged in Cabinet that this 'third force' policy was dead.[66] He admitted that Britain did not possess the capital to develop Africa, that there was no political unity in the Commonwealth, that the UK could not supply imperial defence requirements and that Western Europe could not defend itself without American assistance. Fortunately, he added, it was usually possible to reconcile American and British views as the former evolved, under the burden of world responsibilities, to see that 'the UK and the Commonwealth, and to a lesser extent the Western Continental Europe, are essential to her defence and safety'. This is as near as the British decision-makers came, in the lifetime of the Labour government, to accepting that Attlee had been right in 1946 when he questioned the policy of the Foreign Office and Chiefs of Staff; Britain was indeed at the easterly extreme of a strategic area centred on the United States.

By this time the United States acknowledged the value to itself of Britain's world role and was prepared to exempt it from the process of European integration. There was another year of financial crisis in 1949 when the UK faced national bankruptcy but continued to spend more on defence than any other West European state. The familiar arguments about the need to hold back the communist threat in the Far East and the Middle East, to prevent the eventual fall of Africa to the Soviet Union, to secure the right to occupy Cyrenaica for another 20 years and so on, continued to be trotted out. The military budget already stood at 7.5 per cent of national income when the Korean War began in June 1950. Under pressure from the United States, the Cabinet now agreed to increase this expenditure from £700m to £1,800m for the year and to £3,600m over the next three years. Soon after Hugh Gaitskell replaced Cripps as Chancellor in October 1950, Britain was asked to raise the projected expenditure to £6,000m, though the Americans finally settled for £4,700m over three years – a disastrous annual toll of 14 per cent of national income. In the event the incoming Conservative government was forced to scale this down.

But the American demands represented the price of success. Britain had struggled to regain its commercial position based on the maintenance of the imperial world role and with eventual American agreement had secured the right to retain the sterling area and privileged access to colonial resources. It stood outside the process of West European integration, its armed forces scattered the globe as befitted a Great Power. It was now in no position to do anything other than support the fundamental goals of US foreign policy.

# Appendix One: British Territorial Acquisitions Since 1763

| Territory | Year of Occupation | Independence |
|---|---|---|
| Aden | ceded from Turkey 1833 | 1967 |
| Australia | penal settlement 1788 | 1931 Statute of Westminster formally recognises autonomy |
| Bahamas | 1787 | 1973 |
| Basutoland | protectorate 1843 | 1966 (Lesotho) |
| Bechuanaland | protectorate 1885 | 1966 (Botswana) |
| British Honduras | protectorate 1836, colony 1862 | 1981 (Belize) |
| Benin, Nigeria | occupied 1897 | 1967 (Benin) |
| Borneo, North | protectorate 1888 | 1962 (Malaysian Federation) |
| British Guiana | captured 1796 | 1966 (Guyana) |
| Brunei, Borneo | protectorate 1888 | 1984 |
| Canada | ceded to Britain 1763 | Dominion 1867 |
| Cape (South Africa) | occupied 1795 | see South Africa |
| Ceylon | occupied 1795 | Dominion 1948 |
| Cyprus | occupied 1878 | 1960 |
| Egypt | occupied 1882 | formally declared 1922; last British troops withdraw 1953 |
| Falkland Islands | purchased 1771 | |
| Fiji Islands | annexed 1874 | 1970 |
| Gibraltar | 1815 | |
| Gold Coast | 1821 | 1957 (Ghana) |
| Grenada | 1796 | 1974 |
| Heligoland | 1814 | exchanged for Zanzibar from Germany 1890 |
| Honduras | 1798 | 1922 |
| Hong Kong | 1842 | 1997 |
| India | 1767, transferred to Crown 1858 | 1947 (states of India and Pakistan) |
| Kenya | 1895, transferred to Crown from East Africa Co. | 1963 |

| Territory | Year of Occupation | Independence |
|---|---|---|
| Malay peninsula | 1874–75 | 1957 (Malaysian Federation) |
| Malta | 1800 | 1964 |
| Mandalay (Upper Burma) | 1885 | 1947 |
| Mauritius | 1810 | 1965 |
| Mesopotamia (Iraq) | mandated to Britain 1920 | client state 1922 until Nasserite army coup 1958 |
| Natal, South Africa | 1843 | see South Africa |
| New Guinea | protectorate 1885 | 1962, UN administration |
| New Zealand | 1769 | 1931 Statute of Westminster formally recognises autonomy |
| Nigeria | protectorate 1899 | 1963 |
| Nyasaland | protectorate 1891 | 1964 (Malawi) |
| Orange Free State (South Africa) | annexed 1900 | see South Africa |
| Palestine | mandate 1920 | withdrew 1948 |
| Penang, Malaya | ceded to Britain 1786 | see Malaya |
| Quebec | 1763 | enters Dominion of Canada 1867 |
| Rangoon, Burma | 1824 | 1948 |
| Rhodesia (formerly Southern Rhodesia) | 1895, under auspices of British South Africa Co. | 1980 (Zimbabwe) |
| Rhodesia, Northern | 1889, under British South Africa Co.; direct rule 1900 | 1964 (Zambia) |
| Rwanda | ceded 1921 | 1962 |
| St Lucia (West Indies) | 1794 | 1979 |
| St Vincent, Winward Isles | ceded 1763 | 1979 |
| Seychelles | 1794 | 1976 |
| Sierra Leone | 1808 | 1961 |
| Singapore | 1819, East India Co. | 1962 (Malaysian Federation) |
| Somaliland (British) | protectorate 1884 | 1960 (joins Somalia) |
| South Africa | see Cape, Transvaal, etc. | 1910 Dominion |
| South West Africa | mandated to South Africa 1919 | 1990 Namibia |
| Sudan | subject to Anglo-Egyptian Convention 1899 and joint sovereignty from 1922 | 1956 |
| Suez (Canal Zone) | 1875 | last British troops withdraw 1956 |

| *Territory* | *Year of Occupation* | *Independence* |
|---|---|---|
| Tanganyika | mandate 1922 | 1962, Tanzania since 1964 |
| Tobago | 1803 | 1962 |
| Tonga Islands | annexed 1899 | 1970 |
| Transvaal | annexed 1877 and 1900 | see South Africa |
| Trinidad | 1797 | 1962 |
| Uganda | occupied 1890, protectorate 1894 | 1962 |
| Zanzibar | 1890 | 1963 (joins Tanzania) |
| Zululand | annexed 1867, annexed to Natal 1897 | see South Africa |

# Appendix Two: Chronology 1914–51

| Year | Principal Imperial Events |
|------|---------------------------|

1914    Northern and Southern Nigeria amalgamated; Britain acquires control of oil fields in Persian Gulf; August – outbreak of First World War; New Guinea and Cameroons captured from Germans; Britain annexes Cyprus; British protectorate proclaimed in Egypt.

1915    Mesopotamia surrenders to British; German forces capitulate in South West Africa; Britain annexes Gilbert and Ellice Islands; Egyptian High Commissioner promises British recognition of 'the independence of the Arabs'.

1916    Allies agree to partition Turkey; Easter Rising in Dublin; government commission proposes 'the rapid industrialisation' of India; British-assisted Arab revolt against the Turks; Sykes–Picot treaty to partition Ottoman Empire in the interests of Britain and France.

1917    Imperial War Cabinet first meets in London; Balfour Declaration on future of Palestine as 'national home for the Jewish people'; Bolsheviks expose the secret treaties of the Allies.

1918    Woodrow Wilson propounds Fourteen Points; RAF formed; Montagu–Chelmsford Report on India published proposing 'dyarchy'; British abandon Home Rule for Ireland; Armistice and preparation of peace terms for Germany. December 'Khaki' election returns wartime coalition. Sinn Fein wins almost all Irish seats at Westminster but refuses to take them.

1919    Versailles Peace Conference; Sinn Fein declare Irish independence; Germany's colonies disposed of; Anglo-Persian Treaty establishes British client state; British troops enter Archangel against Bolsheviks; uprising in Egypt; Amritsar massacre in Punjab; Rowlatt Acts curtail civil liberties in India; fighting in Palestine; Britain at war with Afghanistan; disturbances in Northern Rhodesia and Kenya; strikes of railway workers in Sierra Leone.

1920    League of Nations formed; mandates for Mesopotamia and Palestine assigned to Britain; rebellion in Iraq against British presence; war in Ireland against British occupation

aggravated by sending of volunteer 'Black and Tans';
Gandhi leads the first great non-cooperation campaign
against the British.

1921   Rwanda ceded to Britain; Reparations Commission fixes
German liabilities at £6,650m; Egyptian nationalist uprising;
nationalists boycott Prince of Wales visit to India; Washington Naval Conference establishes ratio of US, British,
and Japanese navies as 5:5:3.

1922   Irish Free State government formed; the non-cooperation
campaign in India begun in 1920 is called off by Gandhi;
Gandhi sentenced to six years imprisonment for civil
disobedience; civil war in southern Ireland; Arab Congress
at Nablus rejects British Palestinian mandate; Chanak
incident exposes independence of Dominions in relation
to British foreign policy; Empire Settlement Act to assist
emigration.

1923   British Empire Conference recognises right of Dominions
to conclude treaties with foreign powers; White Paper on
Kenya asserts that 'the interests of the African natives must
be paramount'.

1924   Britain rejects Egyptian demand for withdrawal from Sudan;
murder of Lee Stack in Cairo; General Allenby supervises
reprisals against nationalists.

1925   Cyprus declared a British Crown Colony; boycott of British
goods in Shanghai.

1926   Imperial conference in London decides that Britain and the
Dominions are autonomous communities, equal in status;
Simon Commission on India's constitutional future
established.

1927   Britain recognises independence of Iraq and Saudi Arabia;
breaks diplomatic relations with USSR over intrigues
against British Empire; Japan intervenes in Shantung,
China.

1928   Japan occupies Shantung; Indian Congress at Lucknow votes
for Dominion status; radicals establish Independence of
India League; Britain recognises independence of Transjordan.

1929   New laws adopted in India to suppress labour unrest;
Meerut Conspiracy Trial opens; fighting between Arabs and
Jews in Palestine; Round-table conference on Dominion
status for India; Wall Street Crash precipitates world
economic crisis.

1930   Gandhi launches second mass civil disobedience campaign;
publication of Simon Report on India; Round-table
conference on India in London.

1931    Delhi Pact suspends civil disobedience campaign; National Government formed in London; Japan occupies Manchuria; Statute of Westminster defines Dominion status; Gandhi attends second Round-table conference in London.

1932    Emergency powers adopted in India, Congress declared illegal; Imperial Preference adopted at Ottawa Conference; Third Round-table conference in London; Persia annuls Anglo-Persian Oil Co. agreement of 1901, but new settlement reached.

1933    Hitler appointed Chancellor in Germany.

1934    Soviet Union admitted to League of Nations; Somaliland frontier fighting between Italian and Abyssinian troops; Japan denounces Washington treaties of 1922 and 1930.

1935    British offer concessions to Mussolini over Abyssinia; Government of India Act introduces new constitution; Italy invades Abyssinia; public outcry destroys Hoare–Laval proposals on Abyssinia; strike of Rhodesian copper miners treated as a rebellion.

1936    Military *coup d'état* in Japan; Germany occupies demilitarised zone of Rhineland; Abyssinia annexed by Italy; Wafd ministry formed in Egypt; British military occupation of Egypt withdrawn to the Canal Zone under 20-year treaty; Germany and Japan sign Anti-Comintern Pact; British adopt non-intervention in Spanish Civil War.

1937    Congress emerges as most popular party in first Indian elections under 1935 constitution and demands complete independence from Britain; Japanese seize Peking, Tientsin, Shanghai and Nanking; Italy joins Anti-Comintern Pact and withdraws from the League.

1938    Britain recognises Italian sovereignty over Abyssinia; Munich agreement for transfer of Czech Sudetenland to Germany; Italy claims sovereignty of Libya, Nice and Corsica; Lord Moyne heads Royal Commission (prompted by serious labour unrest since 1935) which exposes poverty and government neglect in West Indies.

1939    Britain and France recognise Franco's government in Spain; Czechoslovakia dismembered by Germany; Spain joins Anti-Comintern Pact; Italy invades Albania; Soviet Union proposes defensive alliance with Britain; Hitler–Stalin non-aggression pact announced in August; Germany invades Poland on 1 September; Britain and France declare war on Germany on 3 September; Britain declares India at war with Germany.

1940    Churchill coalition government formed in May; Britain accedes to Japanese demands for prevention of war materials for China passing through Burma; Gandhi launches Quit

India campaign against Britain; Britain leases bases in Newfoundland and Caribbean to United States in exchange for destroyers; violent strike on Rhodesian copperbelt; Colonial Development and Welfare Act.

1941    Iraq sides with Germany and demands withdrawal of British occupying forces; British forces invade Iraq and Syria; Germany invades Soviet Union; Churchill and Roosevelt sign Atlantic Charter; Britain and Soviet Union invade Iran; Japanese bomb Pearl Harbor, Hawaii and Malaya.

1942    Japanese take Burma, Malaya and Singapore; Congress rejects terms offered by Stafford Cripps; Churchill and Stalin meet in Moscow.

1943    German army surrenders at Stalingrad; Tehran conference of Big Three; Malta and Ceylon are promised internal self-government and constitutional change prepared for Jamaica, Trinidad, British Guiana, Gold Coast and Kenya.

1944    Bretton Woods conference; Churchill visits Moscow; British army intervenes in Greece.

1945    Yalta summit of Allies; Truman succeeds Roosevelt in April; Germany capitulates in May; Potsdam conference in July; Labour government formed; Japan surrenders after bombing of Hiroshima and Nagasaki; United States terminates Lend-Lease aid to Britain; independent Vietnam Republic formed; Foreign Ministers conference in London; Indian Congress rejects British proposals for self-government; a Colonial Development and Welfare Act provides £120m to be spent over ten years; Egypt demands revision of 1936 treaty with Britain; formation of UN; communist rising in Azerbaijan province of Iran.

1946    Churchill's Fulton speech; US Congress approves $3.75b loan to Britain.

1947    Egypt breaks diplomatic links with Britain; Truman Doctrine announced in March; Marshall Aid to Europe announced in June; US forces replace British troops in Greece; Cominform established by Russians in October – Cold War configurations established; Britain refers Palestine problem to UN; creation of independent states of India and Pakistan; convertibility crisis in Britain.

1948    Ceylon and Burma become independent states; South Africa introduces apartheid under government of D.F. Malan; emergency declared in Malaya; state of Israel formed; riots in Accra.

1949    NATO formed; Benelux countries propose economic union; Majlis rejects deal with Anglo-Iranian Oil Co.; devaluation crisis in Britain; communists take power in China; UN votes for ultimate independence of former Italian colonies.

1950    Strikes produce state of emergency in Gold Coast; riots in Johannesburg against apartheid; Adenauer advocates economic union between France and Germany; Britain transfers Somaliland trusteeship to Italy; Britain recognises Israel; Schuman plan for European Coal and Steel Community announced; North Korea invades South Korea and UN (largely American) forces intervene; national service in Britain extended to two years.

1951    Increased defence spending in Britain leads to cabinet resignations; Dr Mussadiq appointed Iranian Prime Minister; Iranian oil industry nationalised; Egypt abrogates 1936 treaty; Churchill returned to power.

# Appendix Three: Glossary of Names, Terms and Events

**Amery, Leopold (1873–1955)** Colonial Under-Secretary, First Lord of the Admiralty and Colonial Secretary, 1919–29; Secretary of State for India in Churchill's wartime government. Strong supporter of Joseph Chamberlain's schemes of social imperialism.

**Armenian and Serbian massacres:** Russian advances on the Caucus Front in 1915 led to Turkish reprisals against the Armenians. Between April and September as many as one million Armenians had been murdered, tens of thousands were deported (to promote what is now called 'ethnic cleansing') and a further 200,000 forcibly converted to Islam. In Serbia 82,000 civilians died during the First World War (compared to 45,000 Serbian troops). Rebellions were put down with great brutality by the occupying Austrian and Bulgarian forces, with thousands being executed.

**Atlantic Charter:** A statement of war aims of August 1941 containing ideals of self-determination which owed more to President Roosevelt and the Americans, than to Churchill and the British. The relevant passages for our purposes clarify that Britain and America 'desire to see no territorial changes that do not accord with the freely expressed wishes of the peoples concerned' and 'respect the right of all peoples to choose the form of government under which they will live'.

**Balfour, Arthur James (1848–1930)** Conservative Prime Minister, 1902–6. Served under Lloyd George as Foreign Secretary, 1916–19. Responsible for the famous Balfour Declaration in 1917 when a national home in Palestine was promised for Zionists.

**Bevin, Ernest (1881–1951)** Official of the docker's union who built the Transport and General Worker's Union, of which he was General Secretary, 1921–40. Minister of Labour in 1940 and member of the War Cabinet. Foreign Secretary, 1945–51. Firm believer in the economic value of the British Empire and strong advocate of colonial development strategies.

Boxer Rising, June 1900–September 1901: Chinese resentment at foreign occupation led to an uprising in part organised by eponymous secret societies. It was put down by the concerted action of Germany, Russia and Britain.

Bright, John (1811–89) Radical politician, leader of the Anti-Corn Law League from 1839 and powerful advocate of free trade.

Brockway, Fenner (1888–1988) Imprisoned during the First World War as a pacifist socialist, championed colonial independence as a member of the Independent Labour Party and a founder of the Movement for Colonial Freedom.

Carson, Edward Henry (1854–1935) Conservative MP for Dublin University, 1892–1918, and as leader of the Irish Unionists organised the Ulster Volunteers to prevent Home Rule for Ireland by arms if necessary.

Chamberlain, Austen (1863–1937) Eldest son of Joseph Chamberlain. Secretary for India, 1915–17; member of the War Cabinet; and Foreign Secretary, 1924–29 (among other positions held in government).

Chamberlain, Joseph (1836–1914) Mayor of Birmingham 1873–76 and Radical MP. Resigned from Gladstone's Cabinet in 1886 in opposition to Home Rule for Ireland. From 1891 leader of the Liberal Unionists. He became secretary for the colonies in the coalition government of 1895. From 1903 leader of the tariff reform movement for imperial preference and imperial federation within the Conservative Party.

Chamberlain, Neville (1869–1940) Son of Joseph Chamberlain by his second marriage. Conservative Prime Minister, 1937–40, constrained to appease the fascist powers. As Chancellor for the second time in 1931–37 helped bring about the imperial preferences desired by his father.

Churchill, Lord Randolph (1849–95) Secretary of State for India, 1885–86, Chancellor of the Exchequer and leader of the House of Commons from July to December 1886. Made a stir from 1880 as demagogic leader of the 'Fourth Party', a parliamentary faction of Tory MPs dissatisfied with the party leadership. Militant imperialist rhetoric was one of his devices. Career cut short by syphilis.

Client State or Protected State: Formally independent states such as Jordan (from 1946), Iraq (1927), Egypt (after 1922), Iran until 1951, the Sultanate of Muscat and Oman, actually came under British protection. This relationship included direction over the composition of their governments as well as supervision of their external affairs and economic management.

Cripps, Sir Stafford (1889–1952) Solicitor-General in 1930, but from then until September 1939 associated with the Labour Left and the Communist Party. In 1940 he became Ambassador to Moscow. In 1942 returned to Britain and became a member of the coalition government. In the summer made the so-called 'Cripps offer' of Dominion status for post-war India, which was rejected by both Jinnah and Gandhi. In 1947 he became Chancellor of the Exchequer.

Crown Colony: A territory subject to the direct, autocratic rule of the metropole through its appointed officials. The Governor of a Crown Colony is responsible to the Colonial Office, rather than the people governed.

Curzon, George Nathaniel, Marquis Curzon of Kedleston (1859–1925) Regarded as an authority on the East after extensive travels, he became Viceroy of India at the age of 39. Member of Lloyd George's War Cabinet in 1916 and Foreign Secretary 1919–24.

Die-hards: The group of Conservative MPs (shifting in composition according to issue) which resisted reform, particularly in respect of the Empire but also over other matters such as reform of the House of Lords.

Disraeli, Benjamin, 1st Earl of Beaconsfield (1804–81). Tory politician and Prime Minister 1868 and 1874–80. Credited with the discovery of Empire as a vote-winning device in an age (after 1867) of the mass franchise. Made Queen Victoria 'Empress of India' in 1876.

Dominion: Self-government within the Empire was granted to some colonies in the middle of the nineteenth century; its foundations can be traced back to the American War of Independence and the British government's concern to avoid a repetition of the loss of the 13 colonies, especially after the armed Canadian rebellion of 1837. Nova Scotia (1848), Canada (1848) and Newfoundland (1854) acquired the powers of self-government soon afterwards. Most of the settler colonies held this status by 1860. The principal

Dominions in our period were Canada, New Zealand, Australia and South Africa – all, in effect, sovereign states (and reaching full legal recognition of this by the Statute of Westminster, 1931) but closely tied to Britain economically and dependent on its military protection. Such states practised sub-imperialist activities of their own, as for example South Africa in relation to South West Africa.

Eden, Sir Anthony, 1st Earl of Avon (1897–1977) Foreign Secretary under Neville Chamberlain from 1935 until his resignation in 1938 following their differences on policy towards Mussolini. Foreign Secretary again in December 1940 until 1945, when as deputy leader of the Opposition, he became an appreciative observer of Ernest Bevin's foreign policy. Succeeded Churchill as Prime Minister in April 1955 and is now indelibly remembered for the conspiracy to overthrow Abdul Nasser in Egypt which involved a choreographed military intervention by Israel, France and Great Britain.

Fourteen Points: Woodrow Wilson was determined that America's war aims would be based on clearly defined principles which he set out in a speech to Congress on 8 January 1918. The relevant 'points' for the question of imperialism are the following:

3.  'The removal, as far as possible, of all economic barriers and the establishment of an equality of trade conditions among all the nations consenting to the peace and associating themselves for its maintenance.'

5.  'A free, open-minded, and absolutely impartial adjustment of all colonial claims, based upon a strict observance of the principle that in determining all such questions of sovereignty the interests of the populations concerned must have equal weight with the equitable claims of the government whose title is to be determined.'

6.  'The evacuation of all Russian territory and such a settlement of all questions affecting Russia as will secure the best and freest cooperation of the other nations of the world in obtaining for her an unhampered and unembarrassed opportunity for the independent determination of her own political development and national policy ...'.

After listing the remaining points, Wilson added that 'in regard to these essential rectifications of wrong and assertions of right we feel ourselves to be intimate partners of all the governments and peoples associated together against the Imperialists'.

Gallipoli, April 1915–January 1916: British, French, New Zealand and Australian troops suffered heavy casualties (around 48,000 dead) trying to take the peninsula from the Turks – an ill-conceived expedition associated with Winston Churchill, its greatest advocate in the British government.

Gandhi, Mohandas Karamchand (1869–1948) Nationalist leader of the Indian National Congress. Described the Cripps offer of 1942 (promising a post-war change of constitutional status) as 'a post-dated cheque on a crashing bank'. Assassinated by a Hindu fanatic in January 1948.

Grey, Sir Edward (1862–1933) Secretary of State for Foreign Affairs 1905–16 and Ambassador at Washington 1919–20.

Harmsworth, Alfred 1st Viscount Northcliffe (1865–1922) Pioneer of mass circulation newpapers, notably the *Daily Mail* in 1896, which was known for its imperialist bravado and chauvinist rhetoric.

Jinnah, Mohammed Ali (1876–1948) Resigned from the Indian National Congress in protest at what he called its exclusively pro-Hindu policy in 1928. Henceforward the leader of the Muslim League and by 1940 determined to create a separate Muslim state out of British India. In August 1947 he became the first Governor-General of Pakistan.

Law, Andrew Bonar (1858–1923) Canadian-born, Glasgow iron merchant and Unionist MP from 1900. Violently opposed to Irish Home Rule, he was Colonial Secretary 1915–16, a member of the War Cabinet, Chancellor of the Exchequer 1916–18 and Prime Minister from October 1922 to May 1923.

Lloyd George, David (1863–1945) Liberal politician and Prime Minister 1916–22.

Lugard, Frederick (1858–1945) Soldier and colonial administrator, notably as High Commissioner for northern Nigeria 1900–7 and Governor-General in 1914–19 on the amalgamation of its two protectorates. This experience was the basis for his advocacy of indirect rule. He was Britain's representative on the Permanent Mandates Commission of the League of Nations, 1922–36.

Mandated Territory: Places, such as Palestine, that the League of Nations entrusted to Britain (or another Power) to govern in the interests of the local population and with the ultimate objective of its independence. South Africa, a Dominion of the British Empire, was given the mandate for South West Africa (Namibia). The role of the League was utterly toothless in relation to mandated territories and they were governed in the same way as other dependencies.

Milner, Alfred 1st Viscount Milner (1854–1925) Governor of the Cape Colony 1897–1901 and of the Transvaal and Orange River Colony, 1901–5, and High Commissioner for South Africa, 1897–1905; entered the War Cabinet in December 1916 and became Secretary of State for War in 1918–19 and Colonial Secretary in 1919–21.

Nehru, Jawaharlal (1889–1964) First Prime Minister of independent India. Nehru was a socialist and leading member of the Indian National Congress who spent 18 years in jail in the period 1921–45 for his nationalist agitation against British rule in India.

Passchendaele: The Third Battle of Ypres, September 1917. The Allied dead and wounded totalled 244,897 against 400,000 Germans.

Protectorate: A territory subject to the control of another state which manages its external and economic affairs without resort to annexation and the extension of citizenship rights to its people. In Arabia, British protectorates included Bahrain, Kuwait, the Trucial Sheikhs, Aden, Cyprus, Egypt and Qatar.

Racism: The language of race was commonplace in educated circles in the late nineteenth century when the first sustained attempts were made to place the concept upon a scientific basis. The idea that significant distinctions between races existed and that the different states of human socio-economic development were related to these distinctions was widely accepted by the beginning of the twentieth century. Social Darwinist ideas (see below) were closely related to such thinking.

Rhodes, Cecil John (1853–1902) South African politician who made a fortune from diamond mining. Strong advocate and practitioner of British imperial expansion in Africa, including the territory which became known as Rhodesia (Zambia and Zimbabwe).

Smuts, Jan Christian (1870–1950) South African politician and general who fought against the British in the Boer War but became a loyal imperialist thereafter. Served in the Imperial War Cabinet during the First World War and as Premier of South Africa was still advising the British government during the Second World War.

Social Darwinism: The doctrines which argue that societies, like species, are governed by laws of natural selection that lead to the survival of the fittest. In some versions the stress is placed on the competition between individuals within a given society, often in order to show that the unemployed and poverty-stricken are inferior representatives of the race, the future health of which can only be damaged by their amelioration (and continued capacity to reproduce). Other versions stress competition between nations or races (commonly both) concluding that the survival of the nation/race is paramount and ill-served by *laissez-faire* policies which allow a substantial proportion of the population to sink into poverty and want, thus endangering national efficiency (economically and militarily).

Social imperialism: The linkage of imperial policies to schemes designed to address economic and social issues in the metropole. Joseph Chamberlain's tariff reform campaign of 1903, for example, was linked to an advanced social policy, at least in theory, by the claim that revenues derived from a general tariff would finance social reforms in Britain. Unemployment, poverty, low pay, sweated labour and the like (also military efficiency, industrial regeneration and 'racial' survival) were made to depend on a new, improved organisation of imperial resources. Not the least part of the attraction of social imperialism for the political Right was its potential for winning working-class support that might otherwise go to the socialists.

Thomas, James Henry (1874–1949) Labour politician and Assistant Secretary of the Amalgamated Society of Railway Servants. Colonial Secretary in 1924 and 1935–36 and Dominions Secretary in 1930–35. These and other positions in government revealed that at heart Thomas was a working-class Tory.

Wilson, Sir Henry (1864–1922) Director of Military Operations in 1914 and Chief of the Imperial General Staff in 1918–22. Shot dead by two Irish ex-servicemen at his London home.

Wilson, Thomas Woodrow (1856–1924) President of the United States 1916–20 and champion of the League of Nations and of the 'fourteen points' which he put before the peace conference at Versailles in 1919 (see above).

# Notes

Place of publication is London unless otherwise indicated.

## Preface

1. J. Palmer, *Europe Without America? The Crisis in Atlantic Relations*, Oxford, 1987, p. 84.
2. Ibid., p. 82; by the summer of 1966 it had begun to occur to some ministers in the Labour government that Britain might be getting the worst of both worlds. See T. Benn, *Out of the Wilderness: Diaries 1963–67*, 1987, p. 449.
3. C. Ponting, *Breach of Promise: Labour in Power 1964–70*, 1989, p. 229.
4. See M. Curtis, *The Ambiguities of Power: British Foreign Policy Since 1945*, 1995, pp. 146–7.
5. Franco's rehabilitation in the context of the Cold War is told in detail in P. Preston, *Franco*, 1993, pp. 532–624.
6. Ponting, *Breach of Promise*, pp. 398 and 94.
7. See S. Pollard, *The Development of the British Economy*, fourth edition, 1992, pp. 354–75; and S. Strange, *Sterling and British Policy*, Oxford, 1971.
8. P. Kennedy, *The Realities Behind Diplomacy*, 1981, p. 382.

## Introduction

1. D. Held, *Democracy and the Global Order*, Cambridge, 1995, p. 53.
2. G. Clark, *The Later Stuarts 1660–1714*, Oxford, second edition, 1956, pp. 61–2.
3. P.J. Cain and A.G. Hopkins, *British Imperialism: Innovation and Expansion, 1688–1914*, 1993, pp. 74–5.
4. L. Colley, *Britons: Forging the Nation 1707–1837*, New Haven, 1992, p. 53.
5. Ibid., p. 52.
6. P.J. Marshall, 'Empire and Authority in the later Eighteenth Century', *Journal of Imperial and Commonwealth History*, 15, 2, January 1987, p. 115. The wars against revolutionary and Napoleonic France certainly led to 'a sudden refurbishment of the symbols of royalty' and an association of royalism and nationalism which was projected abroad in an assertion of the British imperial state in the colonies, against local elites. From this time onwards, as Bayly points out , 'Racial superiority was ... more firmly inscribed in institutions'. See C.A. Bayly, *Imperial Meridian: The British Empire and the World, 1780–1830*,

1989, pp. 109–11 and p. 136. It has been argued that also at home 'There cannot be the slightest doubt that empire was a major component in British people's sense of their own identity, that it helped to integrate the United Kingdom, and to distinguish it in the eyes of its own citizens from other European countries. Empire reinforced a hierarchical view of the world, in which the British occupied a pre-eminent place among the colonial powers, while those subjected to colonial rule were ranged below them in varying degrees of supposed inferiority.' See P.J. Marshall, 'Imperial Britain', *Journal of Imperial and Commonwealth History*, 23, 3, September 1995, p. 385. It is worth adding, however, that while overseas wars and expansion welded Britain and a British consciousness in the eighteenth century, consciousness of a 'great chain of being' with Britons on top of the heap reached a developed form only in the late nineteenth century and even then it is not clear how far the idea penetrated into the minds of wage-earners.

7. P.G.M. Dickson, *The Financial Revolution in England: A Study in the Development of Public Credit, 1688–1756*, 1967, p. 9.

8. P. Kennedy, *The Rise and Fall of the Great Powers*, 1988, p. 81.

9. Bayly, *Imperial Meridian*, pp. 129–30.

10. See D.S. Landes, *The Unbound Prometheus: Technological Change in Western Europe from 1750 to the Present*, Cambridge, 1969, pp. 36–9.

11. Colley, *Britons*, p. 69.

12. R. Hyam, *Britain's Imperial Century, 1815–1914*, 1976, p. 21.

13. K. Marx, *Capital*, Vol. One, 1970, p. 751.

14. Quoted in Hyam, *Britain's Imperial Century*, p. 71.

15. Bayly, *Imperial Meridian*, p. 100.

16. The idea that colonial government provided protection and civilisation to backward peoples grew from the late eighteenth century, as did the expansion of missionary activities with the approval of the ruling class. See A. Porter, 'Religion and Empire: British Expansion in the Long Nineteenth Century, 1780–1914', *Journal of Imperial and Commonwealth History*, 20, 3, September 1992, pp. 370–89.

17. Marshall notes that 'terms like "benevolence" and "improvement" had entered the rhetoric of empire' by the 1780s. See 'Empire and Authority', p. 118.

18. See R.F. Foster, *Lord Randolph Churchill*, Oxford, 1981, pp. 206–13.

19. Quoted by A. Gamble, *Britain in Decline: Economic Policy, Political Strategy and the British State*, fourth edition, 1994, p. 51.

20. Hyman, *Britain's Imperial Century*, p. 13.

21. The young William Ewart Gladstone is an example, making his maiden speech in June 1833 in defence of his father's slave plantations in the West Indies and British Guiana, where slaves were said to have been worked to death and where an insurrection of August 1823 was suppressed ferociously. See P. Magnus, *Gladstone: A Biography*, 1978, pp. 2 and 18.

22. R. Hughes, *The Fatal Shore: A History of the Transportation of Convicts to Australia, 1787–1868*, 1988.

23. Hyam, *Britain's Imperial Century*, p. 37.

24. P. Kennedy, *The Rise and Fall of British Naval Mastery*, third edition, 1991, p. 177.
25. Ibid., p. 185.

## Chapter 1

1. On the imperial military contribution see F.W. Perry, *The Commonwealth Armies: Manpower and Organisation in Two World Wars*, Manchester, 1988 and for the record of imperial conflict see L. James, *Imperial Rearguard: Wars of Empire 1919–1985*, 1988.
2. B. Porter, *The Lion's Share: A Short History of British Imperialism, 1850–1983*, 1984, p. 236.
3. R. Pound and G. Harmsworth, *Northcliffe*, 1959, pp. 206–7.
4. J.A. Schumpeter, *Imperialism and Social Classes*, 1919 and Oxford, 1951, p. 13.
5. E. Hobsbawm, *The Age of Imperialism*, 1987, p. 152; E. Halevy, *Imperialism and the Rise of Labour, 1895–1905*, 1961, p. 53. See also B. Shephard, 'Showbiz Imperialism: The Case of Peter Lobengula', in J.M. McKenzie (ed.), *Imperialism and Popular Culture*, Manchester, 1986.
6. G.R. Searle, *The Quest for National Efficiency: A Study in British Politics and British Political Thought 1899–1914*, Oxford, 1971, p. 96.
7. P. Kennedy, *The Rise of the Anglo-German Naval Antagonism, 1860–1914*, 1980, p. 308.
8. Ibid., p. 58.
9. K. Marx, *New York Daily Tribune*, 21 September 1857, quoted in L.E. Davis and R.A. Huttenback, *Mammon and the Pursuit of Empire*, Cambridge, 1988, p. 262.
10. Kennedy, *Rise of the Anglo-German Naval Antagonism*, p. 410; See also R.J. Skidelsky, 'Retreat From Leadership: The Evolution of British Economic Foreign Policy, 1870–1939', in B.M. Rowland (ed.), *Balance of Power or Hegemony?: The Inter-War Monetary System*, New York, 1976, pp. 164–78.
11. B. Semmel, *The Rise of Free Trade Imperialism*, Cambridge, 1970, pp. 216–17.
12. M. Gilbert, *First World War*, 1994, pp. 33–4.
13. Ibid., p. 155.
14. W.D. Smith, *The Ideological Origins of Nazi Imperialism*, Oxford, 1986, pp. 166–71.
15. L. Macdonald, review of M. Gilbert's *First World War* in the *Sunday Times*,18 September 1994.

## Chapter 2

1. R. Blake, *The Decline of Power*, 1985, p. 67.
2. T.O. Lloyd, *Empire, Welfare State, Europe: English History 1906–1992*, Oxford, fourth edition, 1993, pp. 95–6.
3. J.M. Keynes, *Economic Consequences of the Peace*, (1919) in *Collected Works*, Vol. 2, 1971, pp. xxv and 7.

4. Arno J. Mayer, Political *Origins of the New Diplomacy, 1917–1918*, New Haven, 1959, p. 16.
5. C.S. Maier, *Recasting Bourgeois Europe*, Princeton, 1975, p. 137.
6. B. Porter, *The Lion's Share*, 1984, p. 242.
7. A. Hourani, *A History of the Arab Peoples*, 1991, p. 317.
8. E. Kedourie, *England and the Middle East*, 1956, pp. 35–40.
9. S.H. Zebel, *Balfour: A Political Biography*, Cambridge, 1973, pp. 246–7.
10. V. Kiernan, *America: The New Imperialism*, 1978, pp. 158–9.
11. D.H. Aldcroft, *From Versailles to Wall Street 1919–1929*, Harmondsworth, 1987, p. 23.
12. R.F. Holland, *Pursuit of Greatness*, 1991, p. 89.
13. R.F. Foster, *Modern Ireland 1600–1972*, Harmondsworth, 1989, p. 491.
14. B. Porter, *Britannia's Burden*, 1994, p. 185; Curzon's view of the world in 1919 is quoted in D. Gilmour, *Curzon*, 1994, p. 512; Balfour's is in L. James, *The Rise and Fall of the British Empire*, 1994, p. 371.
15. D. Williamson, *War and Peace: International Relations 1914–1945*, 1994, p. 29.
16. D. Cannadine, *Aspects of Aristocracy*, New Haven, 1994, p. 149.
17. Aldcroft, *From Versailles to Wall Street*, p. 47.
18. P. Kennedy, *The Realities Behind Diplomacy*, 1981, p. 211.
19. M. Gilbert, *World in Torment: Winston S. Churchill 1917–1922*, 1975, pp. 226–51.
20. Ibid., p. 305.
21. Ibid., p. 307.
22. C. Keeble, *Britain and the Soviet Union, 1917–1989*, 1990, pp. 77–8.
23. R.F. Holland, *Pursuit of Greatness*, p. 107.
24. C. Keeble, *Britain and the Soviet Union*, pp. 82–3.
25. Ibid., pp. 102–3.
26. Ibid., p. 107.
27. J. Ramsden, *The Age of Balfour and Baldwin*, 1978, p. 123.
28. Ibid., p. 139.
29. E. Kedourie, *England and the Middle East*, p. 193; see also D.E. Omiss, *Air Power and Colonial Control*, Manchester, 1990.
30. V. Kiernan, *European Empires from Conquest to Collapse*, Leicester, 1982, p. 195.
31. B.Wasserstein, review of L. James, *Imperial Warrior*, in *London Review of Books*, 23 September 1993.
32. E. Monroe, *Britain's Moment in the Middle East, 1914–56*, 1963, p. 80.
33. C. Ponting, *Churchill*, 1994, p. 258.
34. Kiernan, *European Empires*, p. 200.
35. Ibid., pp. 198–200.
36. M. Kitson and S. Solomon, *Protectionism and Economic Revival: The British Inter-war Economy*, Cambridge, 1990, pp. 2–5.
37. L.S. Amery, *My Political Life*, Vol. 2, 1953, pp. 471–2.
38. P.J. Cain and A.G. Hopkins, *British Imperialism: Crisis and Deconstruction, 1914–1990*, 1993, p. 202.
39. F. Lugard, *The Dual Mandate in British Tropical Africa*, 1922, pp. 617–19.

40. Salisbury's opinion of the Indian princes is quoted in R. Blake, *Disraeli*, 1966, pp. 562–3. The negative consequences of tribe-formation under the impact of imperialism are discussed in A.Wirz, 'Imperialism and State Formation in Africa', in W.J. Mommsen and J. Osterhammel, *Imperialism and After: Continuities and Discontinuities*, 1986, pp. 125–9. See also B. Davidson, *The Black Man's Burden*, 1992, ch. 4.

41. Monroe, *Britain's Moment in the Middle East*, p. 82.

42. F. Halliday, *Arabia Without Sultans*, Harmondsworth, 1974, pp. 274–6.

43. B. Davidson, *The Black Man's Burden*, pp. 41–8.

44. H.S. Wilson, *African Decolonisation*, 1994, pp. 11–12.

45. Ibid., p. 25.

46. B. Berman, *Control and Crisis in Colonial Kenya*, 1990, p. 141.

47. Ibid., p. 131.

48. Ibid., p. 154.

49. Ibid., p. 204.

50. M. Beloff, *Wars and Welfare: Britain 1914–45*, 1984, p. 4.

51. J.M. McKenzie (ed.), *Imperialism and Popular Culture*, Manchester, 1986.

52. F. Coetze, *For Party or Country: Nationalism and the Dilemmas of Popular Conservatism in Edwardian England*, Oxford, 1990.

53. J. Morris, *Farewell the Trumpets*, Harmondsworth, 1979, p. 308.

54. C. Barnett, *The Collapse of British Power*, Gloucester, 1984, p. 183.

55. Morris, *Farewell the Trumpets*, p. 314.

56. Barnett, *The Collapse of British Power*, p. 203.

57. Ibid., p. 262.

58. W.G. Beasley, *Japanese Imperialism*, Oxford, 1987, p. 14.

59. T. Jones, *Whitehall Diary*, ed. K. Middlemas, Vol. 2, Oxford, 1969, p. 177.

60. D. Dimbleby and D. Reynolds, *An Ocean Apart*, 1988, pp. 98–101.

## Chapter 3

1. P.S. Gupta, *Imperialism and the British Labour Movement, 1914–64*, 1975, p. 131.

2. J. Callaghan, 'The Communists and the Colonies', in G. Andrews, N. Fishman, and K. Morgan (eds), *Opening the Books: Essays on the Social and Cultural History of the British Communist Party*, 1995, pp. 4–22. The Meerut Trial was held during the life of the Labour government and involved the prosecution of 32 defendants, many of them communists, who were charged with 'seeking to deprive the King-Emperor of his sovereignty of India'; they had been trying to establish trade unions and peasant parties in India.

3. D. Goldsworthy, *Colonial Issues in British Politics, 1945–61*, Oxford, p. 115.

4. Gupta, *Imperialism* p. 118.

5. S. McIntyre, *Imperialism and the British Labour Movement in the 1920s*, 1975, p. 16.

6. A. Bullock, *Ernest Bevin: Foreign Secretary*, Oxford, 1983, p. 114.

7.  C.P. Kindleberger, *The World in Depression, 1929–39*, Harmondsworth, 1987, p. 9.

8.  G. Ingham, *Capitalism Divided? The City and Industry in British Social Development*, 1984, p. 184.

9.  R.P. Dutt, *India Today*, 1940, p. 101.

10.  C. Barnett, *The Collapse of British Power*, Gloucester, 1984, p. 139.

11.  D. Cannadine, *The Decline and Fall of the British Aristocracy*, Yale, 1990, pp. 264–74.

12.  See J. Schumpeter, *Imperialism and Social Classes*, 1919 and Oxford 1951; Schumpeter nevertheless saw 'much truth' in the Marxist theory of imperialism 'as the reflex of the interests of the capitalist upper stratum'.

13.  Cannadine, *Decline and Fall*, pp. 280–81.

14.  J.K. Galbraith, *The Culture of Contentment*, Harmondsworth, 1993, ch. 9.

15.  Cannadine, *Decline and Fall*, p. 283.

16.  S. Bok, *Secrets: On the Ethics of Concealment and Revelation*, Oxford, 1982, ch. 12.

17.  Cannadine, *Decline and Fall*, p. 588.

18.  C. Hughes, 'A Provenance of Proconsuls', *Journal of Imperial and Commonwealth History*, 4, 1975.

19.  P.J. Cain and A.G. Hopkins, *British Imperialism: Crisis and Deconstruction, 1914–1990*, 1993, p. 44. The economic costs and benefits of Empire are still subject to dispute. L.E. Davis and R.A. Huttenback, in *Mammon and the Pursuit of Empire*, Cambridge, 1988, and P.K. O'Brien in 'The Costs and Benefits of British Imperialism', *Past and Present*, 120, 1988, pp. 163–200 argue that it distorted defence spending and drew capital away from Britain. Corelli Barnett takes a similar view in *The Collapse of British Power, The Audit of War* and *The Lost Victory*, 1995, to the extent that he sees the Empire as a strategic liability uselessly subsidised by Britain. Barnett's inclination to dismiss Empire as a case of folie de grandeur is of course completely innocent of any sense of the economic interests in Empire located in Britain. But aspects of his argument concerning its alleged military burden can also be questioned. For this see P. Kennedy, 'Debate: The Costs and Benefits of British Imperialism, 1846–1914', *Past and Present*, 125, 1989, pp. 186–92.

    Particular interests – from individuals to companies, industries and regions of Britain – certainly benefited from Empire. D.A. Farnie, *The English Cotton Industry and the World Market, 1815–1896*, Oxford, 1979 is a good study of an obvious example. W.E. Gladstone, the Liberal Prime Minister is perhaps a less obvious example, given his later reputation as an anti-imperialist. In fact Gladstone retained a personal stake in Empire – as so many others of his class – throughout his long life. In 1882 when he gave the orders to bombard Alexandria he was one of the bondholders that his action was designed to assist, causing his biographer to remark on 'the inherent, almost unselfconscious relationship of capital and imperial policy'. See H.C.G. Matthew, *Gladstone 1875–1898*, Oxford, 1995, pp. 135–7.

20.  J. Morris, *Farewell the Trumpets*, Harmondsworth, 1979, p. 277.

21. Ingham, *Capitalism Divided?*, p. 123.
22. Ibid., pp. 123–4.
23. Dutt, *India Today*, p. 162.
24. Cain and Hopkins, *British Imperialism*, p. 173.
25. Ibid., p. 176.
26. B. Davidson, *Africa in Modern History*, Harmondsworth, 1978, p. 126.
27. L. Hannah, *The Rise of the Corporate Economy*, 1976, pp. 117–18.
28. C.Wurm, *Business, Politics and International Relations: Steel, Cotton and International Cartels in British Politics, 1924–39*, Cambridge, 1993, pp. 289–98.
29. W.G. Beasley, *The Rise of Modern Japan*, 1990, pp. 172–3.
30. D.J.K. Peukert, *The Weimar Republic*, Harmondsworth, 1993, p. 249.
31. T. Rooth, *British Protectionism and the International Economy*, Cambridge, 1993, p. 47.
32. A. Chisholm and M. Davie, *Beaverbrook*, 1992, pp. 301–2.
33. Ibid., p. 310.
34. I.M. Drummond (ed.), *British Economic Policy and the Empire 1919–39*, 1972, p. 102.
35. Cain and Hopkins, *British Imperialism*, pp. 83–93.
36. Ibid., p. 87.
37. M. Kitson and S. Solomon, *Protectionism and Economic Revival: The British Inter-War Economy*, Cambridge, 1990, p. 100.
38. See A.J. Crozier, *Appeasement and Germany's Last Bid for Colonies*, 1988; and R.A.C. Parker, *Chamberlain and Appeasement: British Policy and the Coming of the Second World War*, 1993.
39. B. Chandra et al., *India's Struggle for Freedom*, Harmondsworth, 1989, p. 263.
40. Chisholm and Davie, *Beaverbrook*, p. 288.
41. Dutt, *India Today*, p. 439.
42. C. Ponting, *Churchill*, 1994, p. 341.
43. J. Barnes and D. Nicholson (eds), *The Empire at Bay: The Leo Amery Diaries 1929–45*, 1988, p. 48.
44. D. Low, *Eclipse of Empire*, Cambridge, 1991, p. 62.
45. Ponting, *Churchill*, pp. 349 and 355.
46. Ibid., p. 350.
47. D. Cannadine, *Aspects of Aristocracy*, Yale, 1994, p. 158.
48. Low, *Eclipse of Empire*, p. 64.
49. Davidson, *Africa in Modern History*, p. 118.
50. I. Wallerstein, *Historical Capitalism*, 1983, pp. 35–40.
51. H.S. Wilson, *African Decolonisation*, 1994, p. 35.
52. P. Fryer, *Black People in the British Empire*, 1988, p. 35.
53. Wilson, *African Decolonisation*, p. 33.
54. Cain and Hopkins, *British Imperialism*, pp. 224–5.
55. B. Berman, *Control and Crisis in Colonial Kenya*, 1990, p. 193, note 109.
56. Drummond, *British Economic Policy*, pp. 47–8.
57. B. Porter, *The Lion's Share*, 1984, p. 281.
58. Beasley, *The Rise of Modern Japan*, pp. 176–7.
59. F. Furedi, *Colonial Wars and the Politics of Third World Nationalism*, 1994, pp. 66–7.

60. Fryer, *Black People in the British Empire*, pp. 102–6.
61. Ibid., pp. 30–32.
62. P. Weiler, *British Labour and the Cold War*, Stanford, 1988, pp. 36–52.
63. Barnett, *Collapse of British Power*, p. 375.
64. D. Reynolds, *Britannia Overruled: British Policy and World Power in the Twentieth Century*, 1991, pp. 125–6; see also P. Kennedy, 'Strategy Versus Finance in Twentieth Century Britain', in his *Strategy and Diplomacy 1870–1945*, 1983, pp. 87–109.
65. C. Keeble, *Britain and the Soviet Union, 1917–89*, 1990, p. 120.
66. E.J. Hobsbawm, *The Age of Extremes*, 1994, p. 150.
67. Keeble, *Britain and the Soviet Union*, p. 126.
68. Barnett, *Collapse of British Power*, pp. 439–440.
69. Furedi, *Colonial Wars*, p. 28.
70. Barnett, *Collapse of British Power*, pp. 439–40.
71. R. Ovendale, *Appeasement and the English-speaking World*, Cardiff, 1975; see also J.M. McCarthy, 'Australia and Imperial Defence: Co-operation and Conflict, 1918–1939', *Australian Journal of Politics and History*, 17, 1971. The Australian Prime Minister, Joseph Lyons, proposed a Pacific defence treaty with the United States in 1937 as a means of obtaining the protection which Britain obviously could not provide, but Sir Anthony Eden dismissed the idea out of hand as an admission of Britain's incapacity to defend its Empire – the illusion evidently being as important as the substance. See L. James, *The Rise and Fall of the British Empire*, p. 472.

## Chapter 4

1. CAB 66/1 WP(39)15, 'Financial Policy. The Exchange Position: Inflation', 8 September 1939, a memorandum from the Chancellor, Sir John Simon.
2. C. Barnett, *The Audit of War*, 1986, pp. 159–87.
3. Quoted in B. Chandra et al., *India's Struggle for Freedom*, Harmondsworth, 1989, p. 449.
4. C. Thorne, *Allies of a Kind*, 1978, pp. 5 and 7.
5. C. Ponting, *Churchill*, 1994, pp. 697–8.
6. R.P. Dutt, 'India – What Must Be Done', *Labour Monthly*, Sept. 1942, p. 259.
7. Quoted in Chandra, *India's Struggle for Freedom*, p. 460.
8. Quoted in J. Akbar, *Nehru: The Making of India*, Harmondsworth, 1989, p. 360.
9. Thorne, *Allies of a Kind*, p. 61.
10. W.R. Louis, *Imperialism at Bay, 1941–45*, Oxford, 1977, pp. 33, 192–3.
11. Ibid., pp. 212 and 15–17; see also T. Burridge, *Clement Attlee: A Political Biography*, 1985.
12. Quoted in Thorne, *Allies of a Kind*, p. 209.
13. Louis, *Imperialism At Bay*, p. 464.
14. Quoted in J.P.D. Dunbabin, *The Post-Imperial Age: The Great Powers and the Wider World*, 1994, p. 26.

15. R. Hyam (ed.), *British Documents on the End of Empire*, Series A, Vol. 2, *The Labour Government and the End of Empire*, 1992, p. 168.
16. Quoted in B.R. Tomlinson, *The Political Economy of the Raj*, 1979, p. 142.
17. F. Hutchins, 'India Leaves Britain', in T. Smith (ed.), *The End of the European Empires: Decolonisation After World War Two*, 1975, pp. 35–6.
18. Grand Council Minutes, Federation of British Industries, 15 April 1942, MSS 200/F/1/1/, Vol. 4; and FBI Colonial Economic Advisory Council Minutes, MSS 200/f/3/e1/14/2, Modern Records Centre, University of Warwick.
19. F.L. Block, *The Origins of International Economic Disorder*, Los Angeles, 1977, pp. 57–8; on US policy in Latin America see R. Miller, *Britain and Latin America in the Nineteenth and Twentieth Centuries*, 1993, p. 225; the FBI Grand Council reported that 'almost the whole of the Central and South American market was being lost ... [and] inevitably become the province of US manufacturers'. Grand Council Minutes, 8 October 1941.
20. Louis, *Imperialism at Bay*, p. 51; on Hailey's *Native Administration and Political Development in British Tropical Africa*, 1942, see C. Pratt, 'Colonial Governments and the Transfer of Power in East Africa', in P. Gifford and W.M. Louis (eds), *The Transfer of Power in Africa*, 1982, pp. 250–4.
21. B. Porter, *The Lion's Share: A Short History of British Imperialism, 1850–1983*, second edition, 1984, pp. 305–7.
22. J.G. Darwin, *Britain and Decolonisation*, 1988, p. 48.
23. M. Crowder, 'The Second World War', in M. Crowder (ed.), *The Cambridge History of Africa*, Vol. 8, 1940–75, Cambridge, 1984, p. 33.
24. Ibid., p. 33.
25. Ibid., pp. 34–5.
26. D. Silverfarb, *The Twilight of British Ascendancy in the Middle East*, New York, 1994, p. 19.
27. Tomlinson, *The Political Economy of the Raj*, p. 94.
28. J. Barnes and D. Nicholson (eds), *The Empire at Bay: The Leo Amery Diaries, 1929–1945*, 1988, p. 910.
29. Ibid., p. 912.
30. Quoted in Ponting, *Churchill*, p. 699.
31. Quoted in Akbar, *Nehru*, p. 363.
32. A.C. Gilpin, *India's Sterling Balances*, Fabian Society, Research Series No. 112, June 1946, p. 5.
33. G. Kolko, *The Politics of War: The World and United States Foreign Policy, 1943–1945*, New York, 1970, p. 291.
34. Amery is quoted in Barnes and Nicholson, *The Empire at Bay*, p. 1053; the Colonial Office official, Christopher Eastwood, is quoted in W.R. Louis and R. Robinson, 'The United States and the Liquidation of the British Empire in Tropical Africa', in Gifford and Louis (eds), *The Transfer of Power in Africa*, pp. 34–5.
35. The businessman was Lamar Fleming Jnr, President of Anderson, Clayton and Co., writing in January 1945. Quoted in Kolko, *Politics of War*, p. 294.
36. Kolko, *Politics of War*, pp. 304–7.

37. Ibid., p. 313.
38. See D. Eudes, *The Kapetanios: Partisans and the Civil War in Greece, 1943–1949*, 1972.
39. H. Richter, *British Intervention in Greece,*1985, p. vii.

## Chapter 5

1. J. Saville, *The Politics of Continuity*, 1993, pp. 183 and 186.
2. Ibid., p. 200.
3. Public Records Office (henceforth PRO), FO 371/50912: 'Stocktaking After VE Day', memorandum by Sir Orme Sargent, 11 July 1945.
4. J. Kent, in A. Deighton (ed.), *Britain and the First Cold War*, 1990, p.168; See also J. Kent, *British Imperial Strategy and the Origins of the Cold War, 1944–49*, Leicester, 1993. On the wartime summits see K. Sainsbury, *The Turning Point*, Oxford, 1986.
5. J. Kent in Deighton, *Britain and the First Cold War*, p. 168.
6. Ibid., p. 171.
7. Quoted in F. Block, *The Origins of International Economic Disorder*, Los Angeles, 1977, p. 64.
8. PRO, FO 371 50920: Memorandum from Secretary of State for Foreign Affairs (Ernest Bevin), 4 October 1945.
9. PRO, FO 371/57170: Italian Colonies and UNO Collective Trusteeship, January 1946; Memorandum from J.G.Ward, 6 February 1946.
10. PRO, FO 371/49069: Letter from South African High Commissioner, 26 January 1946; Bevin to Attlee, 9 February 1946.
11. PRO, FO 371/57171: Telegram from General Paget, 8 February 1946.
12. PRO, FO 371/57278: Proceedings of the Second Plenary Conference of the Council of Ministers, Paris 25 April–16 May 1946, p. 103: and CAB 128 Vol. 12, 5 February 1948.
13. PRO, FO 371/49069: Report on Bevin's talks with Molotov regarding proposed Anglo-French Treaty, 23 September 1945.
14. Quoted in Saville, *Politics of Continuity*, p. 209.
15. M. Djilas, *Conversations with Stalin*, Harmondsworth, 1962, pp. 26–7 and 141.
16. W.R. Louis, *The British Empire in the Middle East*, Oxford, 1984, p. 29.
17. Ibid., p. 44.
18. Ibid., pp. 214–15, 307, 632, 640.
19. Quoted in F. Furedi, *Colonial Wars and the Politics of Third World Nationalism*, 1994, pp. 72–3.
20. Quoted in ibid., p. 72.
21. G. Kolko and J. Kolko, *The Limits of Power: The World and United States Foreign Policy*, New York, 1972, p. 66.
22. A. Bullock, *Ernest Bevin: Foreign Secretary*, 1983, p. 15; for an assessment of Bevin more in line with my own see P. Weiler, *Ernest Bevin*, Manchester, 1993.
23. Ibid., p. 73.
24. Quoted in H. Pelling, *The Labour Governments 1945–51*, 1984, p. 124.
25. Quoted in M. Walker, *The Cold War*, 1993, p. 12.

26. *Report of the Office of Strategic Services*, 2 April 1945; quoted in ibid., p. 18.

27. G. Balfour-Paul, *The End of Empire in the Middle East*, Cambridge, 1991, pp. 9 and 14. The figures for oil can be found in Bullock, *Ernest Bevin: Foreign Secretary*, p. 36.

28. D. Silverfarb, *The Twilight of British Ascendancy in the Middle East*, New York, 1994, pp. 52–3.

29. L. L'Estrange Fawcett, 'Invitation to the Cold War: British Policy in Iran 1941–7', in A. Deighton (ed.), *Britain and the First Cold War*, p. 185.

30. F. Halliday, *Iran: Dictatorship and Development*, Harmondsworth, 1979, p. 34.

31. Kolko and Kolko, *The Limits of Power*, p. 312.

32. Walker, *The Cold War*, p. 42.

33. See Saville, *Politics of Continuity*, ch. 3; and R. Smith and J. Zametica, 'The Cold Warrior: Clement Attlee Reconsidered 1945–7', *International Affairs*, 61, 2, 1985, pp. 237–52.

34. S. Pollard, *The Development of the British Economy, 1914–90*, fourth edition, 1992, p. 195.

35. A. Cairncross, *The British Economy Since 1945*, 1992, p. 47.

36. A.C. Gilpin, *India's Sterling Balances*, 1946, p. 5.

37. A. Hinds, 'Imperial Policy and the Colonial Sterling Balances 1943–1956', *Journal of Imperial and Commonwealth History*, 19, 1, 1991, pp. 24–45; see also A. Hinds, 'Sterling and Imperial Policy, 1945–51', *Journal of Imperial and Commonwealth History*, 15, 2, 1987, pp. 148–70.

38. J. Tomlinson, 'The Attlee Governments and the Balance of Payments', *Twentieth Century British History*, 2, 1, 1991, pp. 61–3.

39. K.O. Morgan, *Labour in Power 1945–51*, Oxford, 1984, p. 230; a similar assessment can be found in F.S. Northedge, *Descent from Power: British Foreign Policy 1945–1973*, 1974, p. 221.

40. Ibid., p. 201.

41. D.K. Fieldhouse, 'The Labour Governments and the Empire Commonwealth', in R. Ovendale (ed.), *The Foreign Policy of the British Labour Governments 1945–51*, Leicester, 1984, p. 95.

42. A.J. Rotter, 'The Triangular Route to Vietnam', *International History Review*, 6, 3, 1984, p. 409.

43. D.A. Low and J.M. Lonsdale, 'Towards the New Order 1945–63', in D.A. Low and A. Smith (eds), *History of East Africa*, Vol. 3, Oxford, 1976, p. 54.

44. G. Bennett and A. Smith, 'Kenya: From White Man's Country to Kenyatta's State 1945–63', in ibid., p. 112; the Fabian view is put by R. Hinden, 'Imperialism Today', *Fabian Quarterly*, 45, April 1945 and in A. Creech Jones (ed.), *New Fabian Colonial Essays*, 1959; Governor Mitchell's views can be found in CO 847/35/6, 30 May 1947, in R. Hyam (ed.), *The Labour Government and the End of Empire, 1945–51*, Part One, *High Policy and Administration*, 1992, p. 130.

45. D. Lury, 'Dayspring Mishandled?: The Ugandan Economy 1945–1960' in Low and Smith (eds), *History of East Africa*, pp. 231–32; on Tanganyika see M.L. Bates, 'Social Engineering, Multi-

Racialism and the Rise of Tanu: The Trust Territory of Tanganyika 1945–1961' in the same volume.

46. Low and Lonsdale, 'Towards the New Order', p.13.

47. *Tribune*, editorial, 'Let's Stay in Africa', 20 August 1948; Ian Mikardo's Fabian pamphlet of the same year, *The Second Five Years*, looked forward to the 'joint British–French–Belgian–South African–Egyptian planning and development of the greater part of Africa'; quoted in J.D. Hargreaves, 'Toward the Transfer of Power in British West Africa', in P. Gifford and W.R. Louis (eds), *The Transfer of Power in Africa*, New Haven and London, 1982, p. 134; see also M. Jenkins, *Bevanism: Labour's High Tide*, Nottingham, 1979, p. 70.

48. F. Hutchins, 'India Leaves Britain', in T. Smith (ed.), *The End of European Empire: Decolonisation After World War Two*, 1975, p. 35.

49. J. Darwin, 'British Decolonisation Since 1945', in R.F. Holland and G. Rizvi (eds), *Perspectives on Imperialism and Decolonisation*, 1984, p. 192.

50. Bullock, *Ernest Bevin: Foreign Secretary*, pp. 359–61.

51. Louis, *The British Empire in the Middle East*, p. viii.

52. Ibid., pp. 32–3.

53. C. Barnett, *The Lost Victory*, 1995, pp. 101–2.

54. PRO, FO 371/5666: Minute to Attlee from Bevin, 8 July 1947.

55. Ibid., Creech Jones to Bevin, 12 August 1947.

56. PRO, CO 537/3089: Economic Policy Committee, Practical Achievements in the Colonies Since the War, September 1948.

57. PRO, FO 371/67673: Record of Conversation between the Secretary of State and M. Renadier, 22 September 1947.

58. Ibid., record of Foreign Office meeting, 8 October 1947.

59. Ibid., Anglo-French Cooperation: Meeting of Bevin, Oliver Harvey, Hall-Patch, Dening and Hogg, 26 September 1947.

60. M.J. Hogan, *The Marshall Plan: America, Britain and the Reconstruction of Western Europe 1947–52*, Cambridge, 1987, p. 30.

61. PRO, FO 371/168: Memorandum on European Recovery Programme, prepared for Cabinet Economic Policy Committee, 23 December 1947.

62. Hogan, *The Marshall Plan*, pp. 46–9

63. PRO, FO 371/62740: Cabinet Economic Policy Committee, 7 November 1947.

64. PRO, FO 371/5132: see documents UE 11531 and UE 12502.

65. PRO, CAB 128 Vol. 12, 8 January 1948.

66. PRO, CAB 129/37, CP(49)208, 'European Policy', memo from Bevin 18 October 1949.

# Index